Angela Cavill

The Complete Illustrated

COCKER SPANIEL

Edited by

Joe and Liz Cartledge

With contributions by

JOYCE CADDY
ANDREW CAINE
JOE CARTLEDGE
KAY DOXFORD
JOHN HOLMES
A. M. JONES, MBE
BETTY PENN-BULL
MICHAEL STOCKMAN

Ebury Press · London

First published 1974
by Ebury Press
Chestergate House, Vauxhall Bridge Road
London SW1V1HF

ISBN 0 85223 055 9

Photoset in Great Britain by
Typesetting Services Ltd, Glasgow
and printed and bound by
Interlitho s.p.a., Milan, Italy

Contents

1 The Cocker Spaniel as a Pet   *page 8*

2 History of the English Cocker Spaniel   *20*

3 Care of the Coat for the English
Cocker Spaniel   *30*

4 History of the American Cocker Spaniel   *46*

5 Coat Care and Presentation for the
American Cocker Spaniel   *50*

6 Training   *60*

7 The Cocker Spaniel in the Field   *84*

8 Showing; Starting a Kennel   *88*

9 Breeding   *94*

10 Common Illnesses, Recognition and
Treatment   *116*

11 Kennel Club Breed Standards   *130*

Index   *136*

The Editors

JOE CARTLEDGE
It would be right to say that Joe Cartledge has been concerned with
pedigree dogs and dog shows all his life. Before the First World
War and between the two wars his uncle, the late Arthur Cartledge,
was one of the foremost dog handlers in Britain and in the United
States. It was in these surroundings and environment that Joe
developed his love for the dog game. Except for his years in the
services in the Second World War dogs have been his whole life,
first as a boy with his uncle, and then as kennelman with the world
famous Crackley Terrier Kennels. In 1949 he started his own
kennels and handled dogs for many of the top people in the dog
world throughout the fifties, winning championships in eleven
different breeds, including Dog of the Year award on two
occasions, and Best in Show with an Airedale Terrier at Cruft's,
the world's most important dog show, in 1961. He retired from
handling at the end of 1961 as he found that, with the handling of
dogs both here and on the Continent, his writing and judging
both in Britain and abroad, he was becoming too diversified. He
now judges almost every week in Britain, and has judged in Hong
Kong, Ceylon, Singapore, Malaysia, Australia, New Zealand,
Rhodesia, Zambia, The Republic of South Africa, Brazil,
Argentina, Uruguay, Finland, Sweden, Norway, Denmark, Italy,
Germany, Switzerland and Holland. He contributes a weekly
column in *Dog World,* the top weekly paper devoted to pedigree
dogs. He is Chairman of Ryslip Kennels Ltd., and of Ryslip
Livestock Shipping Company. He edits and publishes the *Dog
Directory* and *Dog Diary.*

LIZ CARTLEDGE
Although young in years, Liz, like her husband, has also spent
her entire life with dogs. She was born in Gothenburg, Sweden, to
parents who were both concerned with the exhibiting and training
of dogs, mainly Dobermanns and Boxers. She came to England
first in 1964 as a kennel student with the Dreymin Kennels of
Beagles, Bassets and Corgis. Later, and until her marriage, she was
on the editorial staff of *Dog World.* A dog judge herself, she travels
the world as secretary to her husband, one of the busiest judges in
the world today.

1 The Cocker Spaniel as a Pet

BY JOE CARTLEDGE

Why should the editor call on himself to write this chapter, when he has never owned a Cocker Spaniel in his life and is not likely to do so? True, he remembers wanting one, as a youngster, but as he came from a family that lived and breathed terriers, this idea was strangled at birth. However, he has certainly been associated with the breed in later life. Having judged Cockers in Britain and in many other countries, he must have handled and assessed a good few hundred over the years. Moreover, after leaving school and before starting his own kennels, he worked and lived with some of the world's top handlers, and for some 25 years has owned large boarding kennels in the south of England. He feels, therefore, that he is now in a good position to give a pen picture of the English Cocker Spaniel as a pet.

Although of course this breed was originally developed as a sporting and gun dog, for many years it has been regarded primarily as a small, cheerful, kindly companion, and also as a show dog. It was in the late 30's that Cocker Spaniels took over from the Wire Fox Terrier as No 1 pet, largely, I suppose, because of their great wins at Crufts Dog Show. From that period on, until a few years ago, they gradually became victims of their own popularity. To put the matter in a nutshell, for ten or more years the breed was mass-produced; anyone who owned a Cocker bitch found it possible to make money by churning out puppies for the pet market. The good, the bad and the indifferent females became brood bitches in the hands of people who set themselves up as breeders just to make a fast buck. The breed was becoming far from what it was intended to be—and thus began its decline. People wishing to keep up with the Joneses and own a dog of the breed that had so many times produced the 'best of show' winner at Crufts found themselves with a pet that had not the slightest resemblance to the active, merry animal they had expected. They had bought themselves a 'gundog' that would run for cover if a car backfired. The breed became hysterical and snappy; soon the word got round that the Cocker Spaniel was spoilt and no longer suitable as a pet.

This was in fact the good news that the old-established breeders had been praying for. The breed was once again left in the right hands, with breeders who had its true interests at heart and knew their job—the business of breeding the Cocker back into the kind of dog which had been used to flush out woodcock, that was good on the show bench, and of such a temperament that surplus stock would make suitable family pets. So they helped the Cocker get over the tragedy of being too popular, and the breed is now again on an even keel.

Pros and Cons
Those of you who are reading this book because you are thinking of acquiring your first Cocker are very wise to consider the matter carefully. We need not go into the question of appearance at any length—this, I am sure, you have already fallen for, and the pictures in this book show it very clearly. In character Cockers are great sporting dogs, more at home, I guess, in the country than in town, and if you are a person who enjoys (or like me, needs) a lot of walking, you couldn't choose a finer or more suitable companion. Being a medium-sized dog, but very sporting, an adult Cocker Spaniel takes a goodly amount of exercise. But even if you live in a town house, he will settle happily

provided you have some garden and live near a park where he can have his daily gallop. The Cocker is a dog which needs much affection; he is playful, and he is easily trained. Like all breeds, he requires firm but gentle handling and treatment.

All dogs must be kept clean, in their own interest and that of the family, but the Cocker is not quite the easiest breed to deal with. His coat, I'm afraid, is so designed as to collect dirt and mud. With a kennel dog, this presents only a minor problem after a day in the field—back into a dry kennel, a roll, a rub, a sleep in straw or woodwool,

followed by five or so minutes of brisk going over with a
bristle brush and comb, and the problem is no more. But
with a house dog the situation must be dealt with before
the dog is allowed indoors. However, a sponge down and a
good towelling will in a few minutes put things to rights.
While on the subject of cleanliness, it is only fair to point
out that the Cocker Spaniel's dangling ears, covered as
they are with long, fine hair, do require extra care to
prevent infection; your vet would be the best guide on the
exact treatment to follow. (See chapter 3, *Care of the Coat*.)

I think I have presented to you the main joys and the
drawbacks of owning a Cocker Spaniel. Now it's up to
you. And if you have decided to go in for this breed, the
next question, which only you can answer, is whether to
purchase a male or a female puppy. The male is in the main
more independent, preferring to go it alone. The bitch
tends to be more affectionate and sensitive, but on the
other hand, she does come into season twice a year. In the
home this can present quite a problem. Over this period,
which usually lasts about three weeks, the bitch can give
off rather an unpleasant smell, and will certainly have a
bloody discharge. She will, of course, become very
interesting to the 'lads' of the neighbourhood, and she will
have to be watched in case these stray dogs get into your
garden. Also it might be difficult to exercise a bitch in
season in a public place. The solution to the problem is to
have her put in kennels over this period, or to have her
spayed; if you have no intention of breeding from her, the
latter is possibly the better answer. If your bitch does get
accidentally mated and you don't wish her to have puppies,
and if you are aware of the mating right away, the possible
pregnancy can be stopped by injections given by your vet.
But these injections will prolong the heat for a further
week or even more. After such injections I have never
known a bitch to conceive on that particular season, even
if mated again, but they will not stop her being interesting
to the dogs. Another point to note, if you've set your mind
on having a bitch, is that there are nowadays 'pills' which
can be given so that the bitch does not come into season;
consult your veterinary surgeon regarding this matter.

There are also some excellent 'anti-mate' sprays on the market, which will take away any odour, and might fool the village Romeos.

Buying Your Puppy

Now, where do you go to get yourself a good, sound, healthy puppy? In my opinion there is only one place, that is from a reliable breeder. Although there are many pet shops and dealers who will try to give you a square deal, a sound purchase can only be made when you know the puppy's true age, and as a rule only the breeder can tell you this. If you have a friend or neighbour with a Cocker who is happy with his buy, and you like the type and general condition of his animal, then go to the same kennels. Otherwise, visit your local bookshop or newsagent and buy or order one or both of the weekly journals devoted to pedigree dogs, *Dog World* and *Our Dogs*. Or you could buy a copy of the *Dog Directory*, an annual which gives names and addresses of most of the reputable breeders of all breeds. Failing this, write to me (at Binfield Park, Bracknell, Berkshire), enclosing a stamped addressed envelope, and I shall be only too happy to post you the name of one or more reliable and genuine breeders in your district.

If you buy from a breeder, it is more than likely that you will not only be able to choose from the litter, or part-litter, but will also be able to see the puppies' dam and just possibly the sire. This will give you some idea as to how you can expect your puppy to look and behave when it reaches adulthood. Be advised not to choose the runt of the litter, the one that is undersized and cowed, and perhaps pot-bellied; the mortality rate of such puppies is very high. Choose the bright-eyed one who comes running towards you. Notice the mother's condition; although possibly a little thin after feeding the puppies, she should nevertheless be fit and healthy.

Buy your puppy from a breeder who gives you the impression that he is willing to offer an 'after-sales service'. Ask how the puppy has been fed, and the good breeder will supply you with a diet sheet. Ask him too about inoculations and worming, etc. Incidentally, it is a very

good idea to let a vet see the puppy as soon as possible, especially if you are a complete beginner at dog-owning and have no one to advise you, so give him preliminary warning, and either take the puppy to him or get him to call on you and give the puppy a complete going over. After receiving a clean bill of health, ask the vet's advice on inoculations and so forth. The puppy should have had his initial wormings, but should there be any signs of worms, or if the puppy loses condition, the vet is your best friend.

Feeding

Because you will have to make some preparation even before you get the puppy home, I give here a typical diet chart, which may help you, though it is merely meant as a rough guide, and where possible you should stick to the breeder's advice, for at least a few months. The chart would in any case have to be modified as necessary—for instance, if you had a small bitch, the quantities might be too big. Again, there might be suitable bits and pieces left from the family dinner (and I don't mean just potato peelings and unsafe bones) which could replace part of the foods suggested.

1. A 9–10-week-old Cocker puppy should be on four meals a day.

Breakfast: Milk (evaporated or Lactol) plus cereal.
Lunch: 2 oz fresh mince, 1 oz puppy meal.
Tea: 2 oz fresh mince, 1 oz puppy meal.
Supper: Rice pudding or scrambled egg.

Add Stress to the main meal (lunch). Give the puppy a baby rusk to go to bed with, or a bone to gnaw.

2. A 4-months-old Cocker puppy should be on three meals a day.

Breakfast: As before.
Lunch and Tea: 4 oz meat or fish and 2 oz puppy meal.

Continue giving Stress at main meal. Replace baby rusk by a hard biscuit. The puppy could also be given a bowl of fresh water.

3. A Cocker of 12 months and over needs two meals a day (some people prefer one).

Breakfast: As before (if you feed once a day, this one could be cut out). 1/2 lb meat and 4 oz meal for the main meal, and a few hard biscuits at night. A bowl of clean, fresh water should always be available. Take your vet's advice on any vitamins to be given.

The feeding of the in-whelp bitch is very important (see the chapter on breeding by Miss Penn-Bull), and you should include a variety of foods—for instance, substitute fish for meat occasionally.

The First Days

When you collect your puppy from the breeder, don't leave it too late in the day, and don't pack the car full of children and neighbours. You will need one passenger, of course, to hold the puppy. Take an old towel or a cardboard box—nursing the puppy in the car will probably make him feel more secure. It is quite likely that the puppy will be overawed by the strange engine noises, new people and so on, so talk to him quietly and calmly. As soon as you get him home, give him a chance to relieve himself, and

Angela Cavill

introduce him to his bed and his water bowl. Remember
that everything will be strange and new to him. It's a big
world, which until that very morning he never knew
existed. He will be lonely and tired. Give him a drink of
milk and the chance to explore his new home quietly
and in his own way and time. What's more, keep those
children of yours from making him into a plaything,
particularly at the outset. I have children of my own, and
I am well aware that yours may have been looking forward
to the puppy's arrival for weeks, but this is not the time to
let them loose on him.

Give the puppy a name right at the start and stick to it.
A good way is to snap your fingers to get his attention and
then, in a friendly tone of voice, call the name—he will
soon learn it. However, even before learning his name, the
first and I suppose from your point of view the most
important lesson is to teach him to be clean in the home. A
very young puppy cannot be expected at once to be clean
all through the night—this is really too much to demand.
But in the morning the first person to enter the room where
he is sleeping must quickly put him out into the garden, or,
if you live in a flat, in his sawdust tray or a corner covered

Sally Anne Thompson

with newspaper. This must be repeated each time he wakes from sleep, whenever it appears to be necessary during the day and last thing at night. He will as a rule soon get the message if you offer a word of praise, saying the same phrase in a kindly tone of voice each time the job is done in the right place. (For fuller advice on house training see the chapter on training.)

It goes without saying that a young puppy needs a great deal of sleep, just like a human baby. Your children must be made to understand that when the puppy falls in a heap and closes his eyes, he must be left alone. If he is forever woken up and played with, a puppy will become nervous and restless.

For the family with only one dog, an outside kennel is seldom necessary. (Unless of course the family is out all day—then I do consider it preferable to leaving the dog alone indoors for hours on end.) The puppy's sleeping bed should be raised slightly off the floor and put in a place out of the way and out of draughts. It should have a suitable blanket that can be washed frequently, or layers of newspaper. A bowl of cold, clean water should be always available.

You will more than likely have a couple or so sleepless nights at first, with the puppy crying out for the company of his brothers and sisters. Give in and take him to your bedroom for peace and quiet, and that will have to be his sleeping place for the rest of his natural life. I am well aware that hundreds and thousands of pet dogs sleep on, or worse still, in, their owner's bed, but it doesn't stop me thinking this practice most unhygienic. Just remember that this pup is with luck going to be part of your life for many years. Maybe ten, fifteen or even longer; that's a long time to live with a mistake.

Finally, let me remind you that just as common sense plays a big part in the upbringing of a child, so it does with a young dog.

2 History of the English Cocker Spaniel

BY KAY DOXFORD

This is one of the oldest established breeds of dog. The first mention of 'Spaynels' occurs in 1400, and there is little doubt that our present-day Cocker descends from those dogs, which were thought to have originated in Spain— hence the name. They were described as being 'of a fair hue', very white, or pied, speckled or mottled. The qualities in them that were most prized were that 'they love their master well and follow without losing him, even tho' they be in a crowd', and that when told, they should go 'wagging their tails and raising or starting wild game or beasts'. Spaniels were used in conjunction with both goshawks and sparrow-hawks, hunting for partridge and quail, and above all, they had to be good swimmers so as to dive and retrieve birds from the water.

Towards the end of the 15th century 'Spanyellys' were still much used in hawking, and in early sporting pictures many little dogs resembling Spaniels may be seen out with sportsmen. They were mostly described as very white in colouring, with red patches, while some were of a 'reddish and blackish hue', which would seem to confirm the view held by many breeders that black and tan is one of the original colours of our breed. (This lovely colour is now becoming popular in the show ring, although unfortunately it is not easy to breed or stabilise.) At about this time there was in France a Spaniel strain of mingled colours inclining to a 'marbled blue and a marbled black'; these, I feel, must be the forerunners of our present-day roans. By 1677 'Spaniells' were described as dogs of 'good and nimble size, with active feet, wanton tails and busey nostrils'.

In 1803 two distinct kinds of Spaniel were spoken of. One was the true English-bred Springing Spaniel, which, had liver and white shadings—obviously the ancestor of the English Springer Spaniel of today. The other was 'smaller, with a more curly type of coat and feathering, and diverse in colour'. This type became known as the 'Cocking Spaniel', as it was very popular for woodcock shooting, and the term led to the present name. It is thought, incidentally, that at some time in its long history the

original Cocking Spaniel may have been crossed with a
Blenheim Spaniel to produce the fascinating diversity of
colour we see today.

In the early days of dog shows the Spaniel classification
was divided into two sections, one for Field Spaniels over
25 pounds in weight and one for those under 25 pounds.
Cockers, of course, came into the latter category. However,
in 1901 the Spaniel Club abolished the weight limit for
Cocker Spaniels and as a result sturdy dogs, shorter in
back, with big ribs and good depth, began to appear.
However, they still showed the same characteristic merry,
active temperament.

In 1892 the Kennel Club first gave the Cocker Spaniel
separate identity in the stud book, and from that day on
the Cocker has been a household word both at home and
abroad. The Cocker Spaniel Club was founded in 1902, and
there are now many similar clubs both in the UK and
abroad; indeed, enthusiasm for the breed has never been
higher abroad than it is today.

We owe a great debt of gratitude to the pioneers in
Cocker history; they worked hard to perfect the breed;
they were courageous in experimenting for both type and
colour; because there were many faults to overcome, they
imported new blood from America to help found new
strains. They saw to it that the breed retained its merry
character, and in the earlier days they still kept it as a
working dog. Nowadays little field work can be undertaken
by the average kennel: to train a dog takes time, and with
the present shortage of staff, it is beyond any owner to run
his kennel, often single-handed, prepare and present dogs
at shows, and also give adequate field training facilities. It
is, however, encouraging to know that the latent instinct
to work is still strong in the Cocker, for many have earned
their qualifiers in splendid style, and there are several
proud owners with 'full champion Cockers'. I myself have
managed to handle one through to this happy position and
I shall always look back on it as one of the most exciting
happenings in the kennel. The field trial section of the
breed is very active; many trials for Spaniels are attended
annually, and the work is of a high level.

The Standard, Colours, etc., of the Breed

The Standard was amended in 1969, and I was honoured to be asked to sit on the committee that proposed the recommendations to the Kennel Club. The details are now as given in Chapter 11.

Few breeds have the wonderful range of colours that we find in the Cocker. The lovely roans, which include blues, oranges and chocolates, as well as the parti-colours and tricolours, are always popular, and are probably among the most interesting colours to breed, since one is assured of getting a 'mixed bag' of colours in nine litters out of ten. Black is one of the oldest established colours, and there are some really beautiful specimens on the show circuit today. Black-and-tans are also coming back into favour, and this is a fine colouring when the tan is rich and well defined. Some years ago one or two breeders tried to establish a white strain, but it was not very successful, and the dogs often lacked the dark pigmentation in eyes and nose that is so desirable in the breed. Of all the colours in the breed I think the reds and goldens are among the most popular, and with the pet-loving public they have an enormous appeal. When a few of this colour started to appear in the early twenties quite a few leading breeders set out to popularise it, and the Red and Golden Cocker Club was founded in 1928. I remember attending the first-ever show held for the colour in 1935 and being amazed at the progress already made. The early reds and goldens had many faults to correct; they had frowns, curly coats and a lot of throat, but as these faults were gradually eliminated, the colour went from strength to strength, and is now in the forefront at shows everywhere.

Recent Developments

Cockers have long been popular both as regards show stock and as pets. Before the 1940 period they were right on top with entries at shows, and after the war both registrations and show entries soared to staggering figures. Unfortunately, as a result of this boom, quite a lot of indiscriminate breeding took place without thought for either type or temperament. Various faults began to creep into the breed, and this somewhat checked its progress. However, there were too many dedicated breeders caring for the real welfare of the breed to let it fall into disrepute, and very soon it forged ahead again. I am happy to say that the Cocker is now as popular as it ever was, both as a show dog and as a pet. There are also quite a few kennels specialising in field trial strains. Registrations are in a very healthy state and the standard of the present-day show Cocker is really good—as proved by the number of good wins in groups, etc., at championship shows.

The title 'show champion', brought into being some ten years ago, has been a great incentive to breeders, I think, although it was frowned upon for gundogs by many 'old hands'. To me it seems pleasant that the Cocker can gain this title after winning three challenge certificates, and thus show the general public at shows that he has won a top honour. It was hard in the old days trying to explain that whilst other breeds had the title of champion, gundogs, despite the fact that they might have won numerous certificates, were not entitled to any title unless they could be trained in the field.

If people who have recently taken up breeding Cockers (or any of the gundog breeds) are anxious to try their hand at working their dogs, there are numerous excellent working dog classes which teach every aspect of field work and hold frequent tests judged by very knowledgeable people. They help owners to assess the progress of their candidates in competition.

Obedience training classes (referred to elsewhere in this book) are useful not only for pet-owners, but also for trainers, many of whom attend to get their dogs on the top line for obedience classes at shows. As the Cocker is by and large a very intelligent little dog, a number of them do extremely well in such classes at shows, and since this section always draws·large numbers of spectators, I am delighted to see a Cocker doing well and proving an excellent advertisement for the biddable and intelligent qualities that the breed should possess.

Children's handling classes are also becoming a feature at many shows, and can prove very useful in training the

youngster in sportsmanship as well as in handling.

Great Kennels and Dogs of Past and Present
There have been great dogs throughout the breed's history.
It stands to reason that in a breed which has been in
existence as long as the Cocker Spaniel there have been
many leading kennels which established strains of world-
wide repute. The early breeders are responsible for the
beautiful dog we know today. Of these pioneers we must
mention Mr Farrow and his 'Obo' strain; these were indeed
the leading stock from which the early show (and working)
Cockers descended. Two other very eminent breeders of the
early days were Mr C. A. Phillips and his famous
'Rivingtons', and Mr Peele, whose 'Bowdler' Cockers also
made history. Mr R. Lloyd's 'Of Ware' kennel was founded
back in 1875 and in due course it passed to his son, Mr H.
S. Lloyd, known to many present-day breeders as the
'Wizard of Ware' on account of the phenomenal successes
he achieved in the breed. One of the 'greats' in this kennel
was the lovely blue bitch Tracey Witch of Ware, who won
around fifty CCs, and BIS at Crufts twice. Exports from
this famous kennel went all over the world. Sadly, Mr
Lloyd died some years ago, but there are still many of us
who miss his friendship and kindly advice.

The 'Falconers' kennel was also a pillar in the breed; many lovely and outstanding Cockers saw the light of day there and went on to win top honours both at home and abroad. The 'Byfleet' and 'Sorrelsun' kennels each added much to the prestige of reds and blacks in the early days, and have been responsible for introducing a lovely type into many of our present-day leading strains. The lovely Cleo of Byfleet was one of the best golden bitches ever seen in the show ring, and Bevis of Sorrelsun proved himself as one of the best-ever red stud dogs, siring dozens of top winners, including amongst others my own Blare of Broomleaf, who in turn became sire of Ch. Broomleaf Bonny Lad of Shillwater, for many years the record holder for reds as regards CCs. I think it is permissible for me to say that Bonny Lad's blood must be behind almost every top winning 'solid' in the breed today, and people still speak with affection of his wonderful personality. Mrs Shirres had a beautiful strain of 'solids' named 'Felbrigg', and it was from her kennel that the outstanding 'Treetops' kennel of Mrs Judy de Casembroot was founded. Few people in the breed will forget the enormous influence this great kennel had on solid-coloured Cockers. Such dogs as the lovely Talkie, Tristan, Terrific and Tenor were some of the best-known members of the kennel, and you will find their names in the majority of 'solid' Cocker pedigrees. We all regret that this very influential kennel is not now in existence. The 'Sixshot' strain is another that has gained much prominence; many famous show champions were bred here in both reds and blacks, and I am glad to say that this establishment is still in great heart. The lovely Sixshot Woody Woodpecker, one of the outstanding dogs bred here, has sired many top winners at home and abroad.

The 'Lochranza' kennel is the home of many lovely Cockers; it was founded at around the same time as my own and is still going strong. The latest black Sh. Ch. Lochranza Newsprint was bred in the kennel and had achieved his title by the age of twelve months. I am very proud that he is by my stud dog Butterprint of Broomleaf. One of Miss Macmillan's earlier stars, the great Lochranza Merryleaf Eigar, who won many certificates, is the sire of my black dog Sh. Ch. Blackbird of Broomleaf, and of many other leading winners at home and all over the world. The 'Astrawin' and 'Kenavon' kennels have both played an active part in the welfare of the breed. Mrs Wise of the former establishment is proud of the fact that she has bred show champions in both reds and blacks, one of the best-known being Sh. Ch. Astrawin Amusing, a black bitch with a charming personality. Miss Mingay's Sh. Ch. Bonny Lass of Kenavon (by Ch. Bonny Lad) also had a meritorious career. The Lochnell kennel has produced a show champion dog in Val of Lochnell, and Mrs Clike's famous 'Gatehampton' strain produced a lot of CC winners. The 'Merryworths', a very old-established kennel, have always been well to the fore with roan and parti-coloured Cockers. Two of the best to come from here were Merryworth Musical Box and Merryworth Music, both multiple CC winners.

The famous 'Colinwood' kennel will always be remembered for the great blue winner Ch. Colinwood Silver Lariot. He broke record after record at the shows, and apart from being a great winner, was also a great sire. Many other full champions came from this kennel, and now that Mr Collins has handed over the reins to his daughter Mrs Woolfe, 'solids' have been added to the kennel with equal success, and many show champions in both black and golden have appeared. The 'Ouiane' establishment is famous as the home of the great Ch. Ouiane Chieftain, a blue dog of considerable merit who has broken many records of late years. Scolys Starduster is another full champion in blues, belonging to Mrs Schofield, who owns the 'Scolys' kennel. He has proved a wonderful stud force, and the beautiful young blue Sh. Ch. Bournehouse Starshine is probably his most outstanding daughter. Last year (1973), indeed, she won the CC at every show she attended. A dog who has done a tremendous lot for the breed is Sh. Ch. Courtdale Flag Lieutenant; a blue of great quality, he is sire of many outstanding winners. Another dog who, besides having a great show career has also had great success at stud, is Mr Weir's Sh. Ch. Wells Fargo of Weirdene. This famous Scottish kennel has bred many grand Cockers. Two other leading Scottish kennels are the 'Nosliens' owned by Miss Neilson, and the 'Glencora' kennel of Mr Auld. The latter owner has won CCs in both blacks and parti-colours, and the Noslien owner in blacks and reds. Show champions have been made up in both kennels. The 'Lucklena' kennel of Mr Mansfield has housed several full champions in blues, and the lovely Sh. Ch. Lucklena Light Music is his latest star; this young dog is the leading CC winner in coloured dogs this year. Mention must be made of the 'Ide' Cockers of Mr Joe Braddon; he made up many champions and show champions when he was showing the breed, and his lovely bitch Ch. Rodwood Lass of Sandover was a leading winner. The 'Oxshott' kennel also played a big part in the history of the Cocker— the lovely blue Ch. Oxshott Marxedes will long be remembered as one of the greats in the breed.

The beautiful reds bred by Mrs Bryden in the 'Scotswood' kennel have gained many CCs, and her leading red stud dog, Sh. Ch. Scotswood Warlord, is a prominent sire in this colour. My own young red winner Sh. Ch. Bronze Knight of Broomleaf, the leading red CC winner for this year, is by this famous dog. Other prefixes with CCs to their credit are 'Craigleith' and 'Misbourne'; both belong to old-established kennels which have bred many leading winners over the years.

I could mention many more, if space were unlimited, but I feel that those I have listed have played a leading part in the fortunes of the breed and should be of interest to all novice breeders—they will help them in the foundation of their kennels and also in breeding along the right lines.

KAY DOXFORD

Mrs Doxford, with almost forty-five years of devoted service to Cockers, seems ideally suited to write about the history and origin of the breed for this book. Her 'Broomleaf' kennel of gundogs was founded in 1935, and up to the outbreak of the Second World War had considerable success. In 1940 Mrs Doxford lost her husband in the evacuation from Dunkirk, but knowing his interest in Cockers, she decided to continue, keeping as best she could a few dogs, which after the war ended helped

her form her great strain. The original and foundation stock had come from the well-known 'Treetops' and 'Byfleet' kennels.

After the war, aided by friends she had made at the radius shows around London, Mrs Doxford helped to launch the Hampshire Gundog Society, which became a tremendous success and is still a great gundog force in the south of England.

In 1947 Mrs Doxford acquired a young red dog, Broomleaf Bonny Lad of Shillwater, after, so she says, 'pestering the life out of his breeder'. He turned out to be a wonderful dog; he was a full champion within five months, and won in all 15 challenge certificates, then an all-time record for a red. As a sire he proved supreme, and there can hardly be a 'solid' today which does not have his blood behind it. He started Mrs Doxford on a wonderful line of winners, and she was very proud to win a 100th challenge certificate this year (1973) at Manchester. 'Broomleaf' Cockers have been successfully exported all over the world.

Mrs Doxford has judged gundogs at most of the leading championship shows, the gundog group at Richmond championship show, and Cockers twice at Crufts. For many years she was chairman of the Red and Golden Cocker Spaniel Club, and she is also a member of the Ladies' Branch of the Kennel Club. In the Cocker world Mrs Doxford is known to be particularly helpful to novices just starting in the breed.

J.C.

3 Care of the Coat for the English Cocker Spaniel BY JOYCE CADDY

Keeping a good Cocker looking its best takes only a short time, but to keep a poor one presentable is a problem— though not an unsurmountable one, if one goes the right way about it. First of all, it is important to know what the coat should look like. The Kennel Club Standard for the breed states that the coat should be 'Flat and silky in texture, never wiry or wavy, with sufficient feather; not too profuse and never curly'.

It may be thought that this is not too explicit. It means that the coat on the body and hindquarters should grow straight and lie flat; it should be fairly dense, to ensure that it is weather-resisting, and it should be fine, not harsh, in texture. Longer hair, known as feathering, grows underneath the body, at the back of the front legs, and underneath the tail down to the hock joint. The amount of coat and feathering the dog carries depends to quite an extent on the dog's function. If he is working regularly on shoots, his feathering will inevitably suffer in the brambles. Most people don't like a very heavy coat in a house pet, and whilst opinions on this differ in the show ring, there is often criticism from the judge if too much coat is left.

In fit condition, a Cocker's coat should shine, and if it doesn't, the reason is either ill-health or lack of attention. A dog that is out of condition will almost inevitably have a dull coat, but there will also be other tell-tale signs, with different behaviour patterns, that will quickly warn the observant owner. A dog with worms will also have a dull coat, and in a small puppy a coat that seems to stick out in tufty patches is particularly significant of that trouble.

The care of the coat can be considered under three main headings: cleanliness and healthy condition; normal grooming; show preparation.

Cleanliness

How often should a dog be bathed? Only when necessary— always bear in mind that over-frequent bathing will be detrimental to the natural oil in the dog's coat. A dog that

is regularly groomed doesn't require bathing very often, because his coat will be kept clean. It is, of course, more difficult to keep a partly white coat looking spick and span in the atmosphere of an industrial town than in the country. (On the other hand, there are fewer opportunities for a roll in the grass on what the cows have left behind, which certainly calls for an instant tubbing.)

Before bathing the dog, plug his ears with cotton-wool—remembering to remove this when you have finished. Don't have the water very hot, and make sure that soapy water never gets into his eyes. Use either one of the special dog shampoo preparations, or one intended for human use. If you have any fear at all of parasites in the coat, use one of the special insecticidal shampoos, or a soap made for the same purpose for humans (e.g. Derbac soap). Work from the head backwards, paying particular attention to the ears. After dealing with the whole body, rinse the shampoo out with luke-warm water and make sure all the soap is removed from the coat. A little glycerine in the final rinsing water will give the coat a nice shine.

Next comes the drying. Unless you take care, this is where you're going to get wet through when the dog shakes himself. The best plan is to envelop him at once in a big towel as he is lifted out of the bath. He can then be dried out either with towels or with a hair-dryer. If towels are used, make sure he is thoroughly dry before he is left, and that the coat is combed flat—if it is left uncombed, in a fluffy state, this can make it difficult to get it to lie flat again during the next few days.

If you use a hair-dryer, it is easiest to work from the shoulders back along the body, combing with a steel comb in the direction in which the coat falls naturally. A fine-toothed comb should be used for the body, and a wider-toothed one for the feathering. When the body coat and that on the hindquarters are dry, use the hair-dryer to blow the hair on the ears, combing all the time, and making sure that the heat is not too great. When head and ears are dry, attend to the featherings on the legs, body and quarters. Again, make sure the dog is quite dry and combed out before you leave him.

Never bath a sick dog; a bitch on heat is best left until her season is over.

There are of course variations: it may be, for instance, that only the feathering is dirty—in that case, only the dirty parts need be washed.

Cleaning without Bathing

Preparations that the writer has found satisfactory for this purpose are:

Foam Shampoo: This comes in an aerosol-type container and must be shaken before use. Rub the lather-like foam well into the coat, then dry with a clean, dry cloth, working over small areas at a time. The whole coat can be treated without getting really wet.

Spirit Shampoo: As this is somewhat astringent, take care to avoid the eyes. Place a little in the palm of the hand and then rub it into the coat, cleaning afterwards with a cloth. This is very effective in removing dirt, especially from small areas.

Dry-cleaning Powder: Rub the chalk-like powder well into the coat, then brush vigorously to remove it. The disadvantage is that the job has to be done out-of-doors, for it is far too dusty to carry out in the house. It is, however, a good way of cleaning a Cocker with a good deal of white in its coat.

Aerosol Dry-clean: This fairly new product is a very fine powder-and-spirit mixture. If it is sprayed on to the coat and then allowed to dry for a few moments before being brushed out, it is most effective.

Parasites

Apart from any other bad effect, these are of course detrimental to good coat condition. The notes below should help you recognise the commonest ones, and you can turn to Mr Stockman's chapter for more detailed advice on dealing with them.

Fleas: Brownish-black creatures, which move very quickly and seem to settle along the spinal region of the dog. They don't actually breed on the animal, but in dusty cracks and crevices, etc., so are fairly easy to control.

Lice: Slow-moving creatures, which both live and breed on the dog. They tend to gather in the warmer parts of the dog, i.e. under and on the ears, under the 'armpits', etc. One type is a greyish-looking insect, about one-sixteenth of an inch long. The other is creamy-yellow, a bit smaller, and creates crusts under which it lives. Both are harmful to the dog's health, as they often serve as intermediary hosts for tapeworm.

Hay-mites (called Harvest Bugs in some areas): So small that they can be mistaken for scurf, but if the dog is constantly scratching and no other parasites are present (especially if the dog has access to a pile of grass clippings or hay), hay-mites could be the cause.

Ticks: Much larger insects, which suck blood from the dog and hook onto its skin with small suckers. The body can be up to a quarter-inch in size, but these are not commonly found in towns.

Regular, thorough grooming should eliminate parasites (apart from ticks), but the operative word is thorough. Parasites tend to appear where the hair is thick around the ears and in the feathering under the tail. If you look closely at the ear, you will see small skin folds under the hair, and these are likely hiding places. If a dog is scratching, it is worthwhile making a close examination. When lice are present, if you run a finger along the edge of the ear, the dog usually gives an involuntary scratch.

If accidents happen and parasites do turn up, don't despair. A bath with an insecticidal shampoo will normally remove them, and if the dog is bathed again in five days' time, this should deal with any which may have hatched out from eggs in the meantime. The affected areas should be closely watched for a week or two afterwards, to check that no further eggs have hatched out.

Normal Grooming

Given a sensible approach from the start, most dogs like to be groomed. The process must be made enjoyable, with praise and reward when he behaves properly. Equally, there must be firmness—never harshness—to make the dog understand what has to be done. Dogs are creatures of habit, and if they get used to a happy feeling of being given attention, grooming will be a pleasant part of the routine for them and for you. Start early, even though a puppy needs less grooming than when the coat is fully grown.

The objective of grooming is to give the coat a tidy, pleasing appearance, to conform with the breed Standard as much as possible without the specialised show trim described later.

The basic tools are:

1. A fine-toothed, short-bladed steel comb (such as Spratt's No 76, if obtainable, or a Spratt's No 73, which is very similar, but has a handle).

2. A wider-toothed, longer-bladed steel comb (such as Spratt's No 34).

3. A brush with fairly short, medium-to-stiff bristles.

Place the dog on a firm table or bench of a height convenient to yourself. If necessary, he can wear a collar and lead, with the lead fastened to an anchor point to prevent too much movement, though unless he is really unruly this should not be needed.

Comb the body coat with the small-toothed comb, taking it through the hair in the direction in which this should grow, i.e. down the back and down the sides and quarters. The comb should be used flat against the body (that is, parallel with it rather than at right angles) and should then remove all the dead and long hair. As you get used to it, you will find that more dead hair is removed with each stroke, and if you place your thumb or forefinger on the comb as it goes through the coat, it will help matters along. Take care, however, not to remove so much that the skin shows through. Stop work regularly and take a look at the results before continuing.

Similar treatment on the feathering would remove too much, so for this the wider-toothed comb is used. Take care to get out all the knots and tangles, and use the hand to feel through and make sure that this has been done.

Finish off the body with a thorough brushing, again down the length of the back and down the sides. By this

Angela Cavill

stage the dog should be in gleaming coat. To complete the picture, comb the ears with the wider-toothed comb, then, with the fine-toothed comb, the undersides close to the neck, and the top of the ears, where they join the head should be combed firmly, to get a short, sleek finish. To avoid hurting the dog, hold the skin firmly with the other hand.

If at any time grooming is neglected, the hair may get knotted in places, and the longer such knots are left, the more difficult it becomes to sort them out. They mostly appear on or under the ears, on the chest, and in the feathering. Small ones can usually be combed out with the wider-toothed comb, but you must be careful with larger knots, for fear of upsetting the dog, and in this case the only solution, drastic though it is, is to cut them out, taking a small piece at a time, using the tips of a pair of sharp scissors, and making sure that you don't cut the skin.

Notes on trimming are given later, under Show Preparation, but the above treatment will keep the dog tidy, apart from the feet. Contrary to what some people say, a Cocker should not have big feet—they should be 'firm, thickly padded and cat-like', and to achieve this some trimming is needed. With the dog standing firmly, use scissors to cut the hair from the top of the foot and round the outer edges. Don't cut between the toes. Pick up the foot and cut the hair level with the bottom of the pads, but again don't cut between the pads.

Sometimes Cocker owners hesitate to venture on show-trimming but want to have rather more hair taken off. This can be done at dog beauty salons, but be sure to give very specific instructions. The normal clientèle of these salons, apart from poodles, expect a short back and sides for summer, and a Cocker is likely to come back minus most of his feathering and with his coat clipped very short. Most breeders believe that clipping ruins the coat, so make it clear you don't want it.

Show Preparation

There is some difference of opinion on the methods to follow, and whether cutting implements should be used for show preparation. At the 1972 European Spaniel Congress a resolution put forward by the British delegation was carried which stated that trimming for show should not be done other than by means of finger and thumb, except for the tail and the feet, for which scissors should be used, and that electric or hand clippers and razors should never be used. The following suggestions are therefore based on finger-and-thumb methods, and if this system is used, there is no doubt that a beautiful and lasting coat will result.

The implements required are as for normal grooming, plus a chalk block.

First of all, it is essential that the owner should have a good idea of what to aim at. Look closely at the top winning dogs at any shows to which you can go. Choosing a time when the exhibitors are not too busy, ask for advice. Study the photographs of the top winners. Remember, the object is to convince the judge that your dog is the best in its class, and by careful trimming to emphasise its good points and make the bad ones less noticeable. The judge will see him for only a short time, and if the presentation can give a good impression, your dog is in with a chance. The work must be started well before the show, but with a little preparation each day, your dog should be ready for his great moment.

Initially, follow the normal grooming technique. Have the dog on a table, rear end towards you. Work from the head backwards, drawing the comb flat through the coat with some pressure, and the long, loose hairs will come out. If you are not yet practised enough to get out all you want this way, set to work with finger and thumb. There are a number of methods. The most popular is to hold the skin between the thumb and forefinger of the left hand, and pull the tips of the longest hairs with the other hand. Another is to make a parting and pull hair along the parting away from you. Or you can, still using thumb and forefinger, pull small amounts of hair at a time towards you. This sounds cruel, but if done properly, it does not appear to hurt the animal or trouble him at all. The use of chalk on the fingers helps to give a better grip.

Use the same method all over the body; if you are systematic, you will work from head to tail. On the head, the skull should be 'cleaned out', particular attention being paid to the back of it; if excessive hair is allowed to remain over the top and round the back of the skull, it gives the impression of a heavier bone structure than is really the case and may also create the effect of a too-high ear placement. Hair should be plucked from all round the back of the skull and a short way down the top of the ears, where they join the head, to get a flat appearance. The part underneath the ears can be done with a comb, but the novice is likely to find this difficult, and may have to resort to thinning scissors to allow the ears to lie flat to the skull. Thinning scissors with one very fine serrated blade and one solid one (e.g. Gotta 65) are useful. Use only the tips of the blades, not the main part; the most common method is to cut upwards against the natural lie of the hair, cutting only a little at a time, then combing it out, and inspecting the result before resuming.

The neck is often quite difficult to get right. The aim is to show up the length of neck and the line of the shoulder —a lot of hair gives an optical illusion of a much shorter neck. Combing and finger-and-thumb trimming here will take some time, but the results will be worthwhile. It is very easy to take too much at a time, so comb out and inspect regularly, and avoid bare patches.

After the neck, carry on with the shoulders, the body and the hindquarters. Remember always the total effect you want, and take out hair in the places you think right.

The legs can be dealt with by normal trimming. With poor bone, obviously more hair is left on. The leg feathering may have to be trimmed, and you must use your own judgment as to how much is to be done. Get a friend to walk the dog away from you and then back to you, to see how it will look from a judge's viewpoint, when on the move. If, when it is moving, any hair appears to be sticking out, or flapping badly, carefully trim out the offending bits, then inspect again.

Use scissors to trim the feet, taking great care to give the firm, thickly padded and cat-like look. I take the hair from below the pads first, from round the outer edges of the pad next, then, with the dog standing firmly on all four feet, I cut off the hair over the tops of the feet. This should ensure that, since the feet are finished while the dog is in his natural standing position, the toes will not be made to look too spread out.

When it comes to trimming the tail, it is too painful for the dog for it to be done completely by the finger-and-thumb method. Generally, any surplus hair along the top can be plucked out, while the skin is kept tightly held underneath with the other hand. Underneath the tail itself thinning scissors are usually employed; take a little at a time until a clean appearance is achieved. If there is excessive hair at the end of the tail, trim neatly with ordinary fine-pointed scissors to the shape of the tail itself, taking care not to cut too much at a time.

Two places that can cause some difficulty in hand trimming are the throat and the hocks. Many people find it too painful for the dog to finger-trim the throat, so thinning scissors are used; the type suggested for ears will give a finer cut and neater finish. Use the scissors to thin the hair in the form of a V shape from the breast-bone upwards and outwards, to cover the area between the breast-bone and the undersides of the ears. Trimming of hocks by hand is difficult, though less so with practice, but the novice will probably find it easier to use thinning scissors. If it is done by hand, it is best to flick the hair upwards, away from its natural lie, and then it is easy to

The American Cocker Spaniel, sometimes referred to as
the Yankee, has been evolved from the same basic stock
as the English Cocker. Up to the 1870's the Spaniel family
was very mixed in Britain, and small-sized Spaniels were
known as Cockers, irrespective of how their parents were
described—indeed, 'Cockers' and 'Field Spaniels' could
come from the same litter. The only qualification for a
dog to compete as a Cocker was that he should be under
the weight of 25 pounds.

In 1879 the most famous of all Cockers was born. His
name was Obo and he was the offspring of a Sussex
Spaniel sire and a Field Spaniel dam, the breeder being
Mr James Farrow. His son, Obo II, was born in Canada
out of a bitch called Chloe II, who had been exported in
whelp by Mr F. Pitcher. Obo II was sold to Mr J. P. Willey
of Salmon Falls, New Hampshire. He was a black dog with
a curly coat, especially on the shoulders and hindquarters,
and also carried profuse feathering; his weight was $23\frac{1}{2}$
pounds and he measured $9\frac{1}{2}$ inches from foot to withers.
Obo II proved to be the prince of stud Cockers. He was the
direct ancestor of Robinhurst Foreglow, and all winning
American Cockers of yesterday and today are direct
descendants of four sons of Foreglow—Red Brucie, Ch.
Sandsprings Surmise, Ch. Midkiff Miracle Man and the
Canadian Ch. Limestone Laddie. All other lines not having
this blood have completely disappeared from the breed over
the years.

Robinhurst Foreglow, owned by Judge Townsend
Scudder, was a dog of good substance, weighing 28–30
pounds. Blackstone Chief, the sire of Foreglow, weighed 26
pounds and was lighter in bone. The story goes that Judge
Scudder wanted to buy him, and in order to do this had to
buy the entire Blackstone kennel of over thirty dogs. He
offered Foreglow at stud without fee to anyone owning a
typical Cocker bitch and desiring to breed to the dog.

In the 1930's the American type of Cocker really began
to go places, and registrations shot up at the American
Kennel Club. Some of the great stud dogs of the period

were Ch. Stockdale Town Talk, a black whelped in 1939;
Ch. Maddies Vagabond Return, a buff whelped in 1949; Ch.
Honey Creek Heirloom, a parti-colour also whelped in
1949; and Ch. St Andrea's Medicine Man, a black and tan
whelped in 1950.

The breed was first introduced to the UK from Holland
in about 1965, but since then many dogs have been
imported direct from the USA. Prominent among imported

stud dogs are A.Ch. Lochranza Evdon's Escort, A.Ch. and Sh. Ch. Dreamridge Delegate (winner of the gundog group at Crufts 1972), and A.Ch. Cholsey's Orients Secret Pleasure.

The American Cocker Spaniel makes a wonderful family pet. His greatest attribute is his merry disposition, and he is very adaptable. He is a great protector and a dog to be loved, and will return this love by devotion and eagerness to please, thus becoming one of the family. The American Cocker takes to obedience training like a duck to water, and if directed in the correct manner learns easily and retains his education.

A dog of this breed should be equable in temperament, with no suggestion of timidity or shyness. Before purchasing a puppy it is wise to see and handle the parents. Many bad-dispositioned dogs have of course been ruined by their owners, but others can be the result of careless breeding.

Prospective owners of a Yankee should realise that with the heavy coat which most of them carry, daily grooming is necessary, and a professional trim will certainly be required every four to six weeks. Failure to provide this will result in a 'woolly sheep', when nothing short of shearing will restore the animal to a clean and comfortable state—but it will be many months before he assumes the correct American Cocker appearance again. Proper grooming will also mean the Cocker never has a 'doggy' odour. The breeder from whom you purchase your puppy will be only too pleased to advise you on the correct coat care and should be able to give you the address of the professional establishment nearest your home where he can be taken for his trim. (See also the following chapter.)

A reputable breeder will supply you with a diet sheet and feeding advice, but see also the first chapter in this book; remember that the Yankee is a slightly smaller dog than the English Cocker, so adjust quantities accordingly.

The difference in appearance between the American and the English Cocker is mainly in the head, which is distinctly domed and has a deep stop; the lips are slightly pendulous, and the eyes are larger than in the English dog, set to look straight ahead, under slightly prominent brows. The American dog carries a much more profuse coat and is smaller than his English cousin, the ideal height for a dog being 15½ inches and for a bitch 14½ inches. When trained to the gun the American Cocker soon proves his ability to work, and already in this country two bitches, owned by Mr R. H. Wylde of the well-known 'Eldwythe' prefix, have qualified in the field, although their training to the gun did not commence until the ages of three and five years respectively. The younger of the two, Eldwythe Enchanto, is the first full champion in the breed.

A. M. JONES, MBE

We were delighted to be able to persuade Mrs Jones to write this chapter for us, knowing her devotion to and keen interest in this breed since it first started in this country. Born in Cheshire and educated in Belgium, Mrs Jones has long been connected with dogs, particularly Springers and various terrier breeds which had always been part of the family. She served in the WAAF (as it was then) from 1939–46, and was awarded the MBE in the Birthday Honours List in 1946. In 1959 she took up serious breeding of English Cocker Spaniels; these were followed by Welsh Springers and Field Spaniels, and in 1966–67 by American Cockers. She imported her first American Cocker from the USA in 1967 and followed this with another import at the end of the year. Mrs Jones is passed by the Kennel Club to award challenge certificates in both American Cockers and Field Spaniels, and judged the former at Crufts in 1972. She is also the proud breeder of the first show champion of the American breed in this country, Sh. Ch. Mittina Kiss Me Too of Spawood. Her 'Mittina' prefix is respected the world over, and many of her dogs have been successfully exported, one of the latest being Mittina Tiger's Tail to Australia, where it is being campaigned with great success at the present time. Mrs Jones is the Secretary and a founder member of the American Cocker Spaniel Club of Great Britain.

J.C.

Coat Care and Presentation for the American Cocker Spaniel BY ANDREW CAINE

When I started in American Cockers in 1967, they were trimmed and presented in this country very differently from nowadays. Some of them looked most peculiar, with a mass of hair very often brushed forward on their heads to look like a crest, instead of lying short, and with a terrific sweep of 'skirt' to the floor, which certainly precluded anyone from assessing movement (although I have in fact yet to see an unsound Yankee).

Over the years presentation has improved very considerably, with a more uniform approach, although it has been difficult to obtain the personal help of American experts, and even now some of the presentation cannot be compared with that seen in America.

For myself, I spent many hours reading, studying the photographs in American magazines and experimenting, not only on a different approach, but also with different tools, until I worked out a pattern which suited my tastes.

I had the great privilege and pleasure of staying for five weeks at the home of Tom O'Neal and his world-famous 'Dreamridge' American Cocker kennels, covering Christmas and the period of intense activity for the Spaniel Specialty show held annually at the Statler Hilton, New York. I also had the honour of bathing Ron Fabis's string of thirteen beautiful Cockers, and helping to prepare them for the ring. Perhaps a little of the experience gained may serve to help anyone who, like me, has problems on starting with the breed.

First of all, a show dog must be clean, healthy and well groomed (groomed regularly, not just on the day before the show, or even at the show itself, as I have seen done on many occasions by people who should know better).

When it comes to the details of grooming, you need to treat each dog as an individual, bearing in mind that no two dogs are alike in conformation, coat and show requirements.

I have found the black coats to be much the most difficult to manage, and they therefore take most time. The buffs are a close second, but I have found parti-colours comparatively easy, as they don't tend to have quite the quantity or density of hair.

Trimming

No coat should be taken off your Cocker unless you have a good reason for doing so. This should mean you only take off coat to enhance the appearance, and not because you get mad at any knots and tangles you've been foolish enough to allow to form. (Incidentally, I have been most shattered when judging to find blocks of matted hair under a thin layer of apparently well-groomed top coat—and this from experienced exhibitors.)

Good tools are essential, and they should be of the best quality you can afford with really sharp scissors regularly sharpened. It is impossible to do a first-class job with blunt blades—they only tear the hair, and what is worse, hurt the poor dog. You will need as a minimum:

Spratt's combs Nos 74 and 76.
A couple of pin brushes—choose the ones that suit you best.
Sharp scissors, with both ordinary and slightly curved blades.
Coarse and fine thinning scissors.

If you are going to do the job properly you will also need:

(a) A good set of electric clippers and one or two different heads. I have an Oster Model A5 with Nos 10 and 15 heads, and an Aesculap 3 mm, for roughing out over thick areas, and to use before employing a No 10 for smoothing over.

(b) A good hair-drier. (It is impossible to dry such a thickness of coat by hand towelling alone.) I have a Solis (Swiss), which I find excellent. It was not so expensive as some larger ones, and is adequate for quick and efficient service. When I first started on this breed, I managed with a Boots' ladies' hair-dryer, which was all right, but rather slow.

With regard to clippers, you must realise that a tiny

puppy has to be educated to take their noise in his stride. I find the best way is to stand the puppy on my grooming table for a short while for several days, with the clippers already switched on and placed a short distance away. I then gently use the coarse thinning scissors just on the face and the top of the ears, to get him used to having his head handled, and of course I brush his body coat. If the puppy is trained right from the start to stand quietly, then you should have no problems, but you must take care not to hurt him and have patience not to hurry.

When you have got your Cocker to stand for the clippers, probably the hardest thing for you to do is to put them away. By this I mean that once you have done the head and ears, and the front of the neck to the breast-bone, you should forget the clippers until the next time they are required. The remainder of the coat should be trimmed only

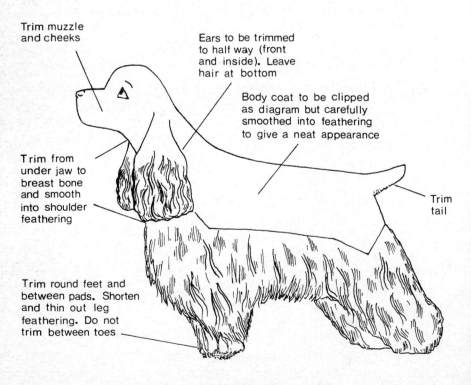

Trim muzzle and cheeks

Ears to be trimmed to half way (front and inside). Leave hair at bottom

Body coat to be clipped as diagram but carefully smoothed into feathering to give a neat appearance

Trim from under jaw to breast bone and smooth into shoulder feathering

Trim tail

Trim round feet and between pads. Shorten and thin out leg feathering. Do not trim between toes

PET OR KENNEL TRIM

with thinning and ordinary scissors, or by finger and thumb.

After the first very rough trim on the head and before going any further, I usually bathe my dog (see below), because I find it much easier to trim him when he is clean; the fur is so much softer. Should I have been careless enough to allow the coat to 'tag', I find it easiest to pull these tags gently apart while the dog is still in the bath (not after drying); it is then not so difficult to stroke them out gently with a pin brush. When the dog is dry I continue with the trimming.

The sides of the neck are thinned and blended in with the fine thinning scissors, and I brush in between times with a pin brush to make sure the neck becomes smooth. There should be a slight inverted V from the base of the occiput, blended into the shoulders and giving a lovely arch to the neck. Don't be tempted to thin down too far over the shoulders, as this will give the impression that the dog is 'out at the shoulders'. Similar thinning should be carried out at the rear end, including the tail, and should leave a neat appearance; don't trim too far down the thighs—and do remember, if you take too much off in the wrong places, it can take almost a whole year to grow right! I personally like to do a bit at a time, and to get someone to 'stand' the dog for me, so that I can look at it from all angles.

I always do the feet last, taking the fur level with the pads underneath, but *never* on top. The completed foot should look like a pom-pom, not a pancake, and very neat and tidy. This is where your curved scissors come in handy for finishing off.

If I am trimming a pet dog belonging to someone else, I leave the ears until the very last because, unless the owner has spent some time combing them, these are usually tagged. If I can, I use a No 76 Spratt's comb by the end, to try to tease out any lumps, but if this upsets the dog too much, it is perhaps kinder to clip off altogether and let the fur grow again, which in this place it does surprisingly quickly.

Bathing

As I said before, each dog must be treated as an individual. Some need bathing the day before a show, some three or four days before, and only by experimenting can you discover what is just right for your dog. The type of shampoo can make all the difference to the texture and appearance of the coat, and since the breed Standard requires a soft, silky coat, it is wise to try several makes to find out which exactly suits. For my dogs, I find the St Aubrey Protein Shampoo excellent, as it does not need a conditioner, but I do use a cream rinse, which is applied, left for a few minutes, and then thoroughly rinsed off, all traces of lather being removed.

I should perhaps mention here that when a dog is being extensively campaigned, it is possible for the coat to become dry, if not properly cared for. In this case a good coat oil, such as St Aubrey's, is very helpful. Since the purpose of the oil is to prevent the *skin* drying, I part the hair and rub the oil well into the roots, and then brush the hair into place—carefully, to avoid waving. There is, however, always the problem with oil that you may not remove it thoroughly, and it will then leave the coat flat and very dull-looking. You must shampoo at least three times, and rinse extra well, until the hair 'squeaks' when you move your hand over it.

For drying I place my dogs on the grooming table. Here the coat is brushed flat, a towel is pinned over the body coat and heat is applied from the dryer. I find I can brush the leg feathering at the same time, and usually in about half an hour the dog is dry enough for me to remove the towel—otherwise the coat may develop an undesirable wave. When all this is done and the dog is dry, the trimming can be finished.

Pre-Show Trimming

A lot of ideas on presentation can be gleaned from ringside observation and by watching dogs which please *your* eye— for no two people see the same things, except in general terms. I would advise studying the people who do the winning in the show ring, and if you are not sure about

certain points, then ask—you may occasionally get your head bitten off, but on the whole breeders are quite prepared to give a helping hand and friendly advice.

The breed Standard allows very few points for coat, but judges and exhibitors do place a great deal of importance on this item, and often coat (or the lack of it) makes or breaks an otherwise good dog. The final trimming therefore should be completed with care.

I myself dislike seeing a too 'sharp' clippered head, so I prefer to do this trimming three or four days before a show, to give time for the clipper marks to disappear.

Use the No 10 clipper head to trim the head, top of the ears and side of the throat to the breast-bone. If you have a dog which won't stand still, it is as well to finish between the eyes with the coarse thinning scissors rather than risk an accident. Leave a slight top-knot, which should be blended in with thinning scissors to give a smooth finish and kind expression.

On the body coat, including the tail, you may use an H7 head on your clipper and work from the back of the occiput, with the lay of the coat towards the tail. Blend the coat into the leg feathering with careful use of the coarse thinners, finishing off with the fine ones; any excess of feathering on the tummy and legs may be attended to, to make the dog look neat. Scissor round the feet.

Don't forget to comb and brush all the feathering, and check that there are no little mats left between the toes, under the legs, etc. These should be removed carefully by ordinary scissors (but be careful—don't cut the dog) and then with a No 76 comb.

After bathing your Cocker, rinse well, brush while blowing the coat dry, and you should have a dog to be proud of. If you have done your work well, he should now need no more attention before the all-important show, except to keep him clean. Don't of course allow any romping in wet grass after all this work; if you have one, a wire-bottomed kennel is ideal for keeping your dog from staining his feet and feathering.

On the day of the show, just before going into the ring, use, if you wish, a good grooming spray, applied carefully and sparingly. Brush the leg feathering upwards to allow the hairs to separate, then lightly downwards, and you should have a beautifully groomed dog. Good luck!

ANDREW CAINE

Although young in years, Andrew Caine is very well equipped to write the chapter on the trimming and presentation of the American Cocker. Born in 1949, Andrew was from a very early age surrounded by pets—rabbits, cats, guinea-pigs, white mice, birds and, of course, dogs. A pedigree orange Rex rabbit provided his introduction to livestock exhibiting and was the eight-year-old boy's first champion. Following this, Andrew bought with his own money a first-cross Border Collie. In 1961 the family acquired a Cocker, and shortly afterwards another Cocker bitch. Successes in junior handling classes came, and Andrew was hooked. Later on there followed more Cockers and more successes, and a great thrill in 1967 when he won his first reserve challenge certificate with his home-bred bitch, Ballantrae Fascination, at the Manchester championship show. At about this time young Mr Caine fell badly for the American Cocker, but he had to wait two years before he acquired his first, Chandhara's So Appealing.

To this youngster it became a challenge to help put the American Cocker on the British map, and to campaign the lovely new breed. Known by his family as 'Fiddle-fingers', because he was always taking things apart and putting them together again, he was greatly fascinated by the trimming and coat presentation of the breed. Endless hours were spent experimenting to improve the appearance of his dogs for the show ring. In 1969 Andrew imported the black/white American Ch. Dreamridge Delegate from Mr Tom O'Neal, USA. Not only has this dog given a lot of pleasure to Andrew and his family, but he has also had a wonderful show career in Britain and is proving himself as a very useful sire. At the time of writing he has won five gundog groups at all breeds championship shows, and, the biggest thrill of all, in 1972 won the gundog group at Crufts. In the same year he topped all other gundogs in the *Dog World* St Aubrey nationwide competition.

All Mr Caine's exhibits are handled and presented by him, and it is small wonder that we were delighted when we were able to persuade this talented young man to put into writing for this book his knowledge of trimming and presentation.

J.C.

6 Training

BY JOHN HOLMES

The first essential in training is not patience or love of animals as so many people think. And it is not a knowledge of how to make a dog sit, lie down, or take up any other position, as some books would have us believe. The first essential is what I call dog sense – a knowledge of canine mentality – giving one the ability to understand what makes a dog tick.

The reason why the dog is so much easier to train than the cat (which has been domesticated for just as long) is not because it is more intelligent. It is because the dog is a pack animal while the cat prefers a more or less solitary existence. In a pack of dogs there is a very highly developed social order with a leader and followers in a very definite order – top dogs and underdogs, so to speak. One also finds top cats and undercats but there is a vast difference. Whereas the underdogs actually obey and follow their leaders, an undercat simply keeps out of the way of a top cat. The dog's natural instinct is, therefore, to obey a leader, while a cat only wants to please itself, which means that a dog can be made to do certain things we want even when he does not like doing them, while a cat can only be persuaded to do things it likes doing.

One of the most remarkable features of the domestic dog is the extent to which it still retains the mental character-istics of its wild ancestry. Man has created a larger variety of canine types than in any other domestic species. It is hard to believe that the Pekingese and the Great Dane, the Chihuahua and the Irish Wolfhound all have the same common ancestry. By looking at them one could be excused for saying 'It's impossible!'. But by studying their mental make-up one becomes more and more aware of the similarity in all breeds. Of course different breeds, produced for different jobs, have certain differences in mentality but they are not nearly as great as is generally believed. It is certainly much less than the different opinions of their breeders. Ask a dedicated breeder of *any* breed and he or she will tell you that it is definitely different from *all* other breeds and of course better in every way. And these people honestly believe what they say for the simple reason that they have never owned any other breed and are so wrapped up in their own that they never even see the breed being judged in the next ring at a dog show. I mention this because I believe that much confusion in training is caused by the idea that each breed has a completely different mentality.

In my time I have trained many dogs for many purposes – film dogs, gun dogs, sheepdogs, guard dogs, working terriers, etc., and I have found that the basic principles of training apply to all dogs of all breeds and indeed to all animals.

The first principle is that by nature the dog wants a leader that it can respect and obey. And he is quite willing, indeed grateful, to be led by a human pack leader. This does not mean that dogs are almost human and it is a dreadful insult to the canine species to suggest that they are. It simply means that we are all animals and many of us are capable of taking on the role ôf pack leader, providing that we are more intelligent and stronger willed than the animal we want to obey us. That many are not is evidenced by the number of disobedient, trouble-making dogs to be seen everywhere.

Here we have a two-way problem. The majority of dogs are what is known as submissive and want to follow a leader but a few are born to be leaders and are known as dominant dogs. Exactly the same happens in the human race and, although we do not usually talk about dominant and submissive people, many readers will know what I mean. The problem usually arises from the fact that a submissive person can rarely train a dominant dog. It is for this reason that a dog will often obey one member of the family and not another. Normally a dog obeys the father first, the mother second and treats young children as equals. But sometimes the dog will obey the mother and take no notice of what the father says. I have invariably found in such cases that the husband obeys the wife too! A dominant person rarely gets the same pleasure from a submissive dog as from a fairly dominant one. Although easy to train to a high standard I get little pleasure from training submissive dogs. All the dogs which stand out in my memory as 'greats' have been dominant, many of them bloody-minded awkward brutes which had been discarded by their previous owners.

This is not a chapter on how to choose a dog but, if you have not already bought one, you should pay particular attention to this point. A person who cannot train one dog may get another *of the same breed* and train it to perfection. Likewise the dog which that person failed to train may go to someone else who will train it quite easily.

The next principle is that dogs do not reason as we do. Here there is considerable difference of opinion. On the one hand there are scientists who say that man is the only animal which reasons. On the other there are people who claim that their dog not only understands every word they say to it but actually talks to them as well, and they carry on regular conversations. Most scientists study dogs under clinical conditions which are quite unnatural. Nothing could be more unnatural than the conditions under which the average domestic dog lives but these are still very different from laboratory conditions, and many pet owners are so preoccupied with turning their dearly beloved into a four-legged human being that they really do believe it does many of the stupid things people do and they never allow it to do any of the clever things which dogs can do.

In my opinion dogs do sometimes reason to a considerable extent. But we cannot really say to what extent and, as the dog cannot tell us, it is unlikely that we shall ever know. What trainers have learned from experience is that to attempt to train an animal is doomed to failure if it is assumed that it can reason. All training must, therefore, be based on the assumption that *dogs do not reason.*

Dogs learn by association of ideas. They associate certain sounds or sights with pleasure or displeasure. They tend to do the things naturally which result in pleasure and refrain from those which create displeasure. I believe that a dog associates sounds and sights in exactly the same way as we do. All of us can think of a tune, the sound of waves breaking on the seashore, gunfire, a police car siren or one of many other sounds which bring back vivid memories –

pleasant or unpleasant – every time we hear them. Likewise with things we have seen and the same sight and sound may well bring back either pleasant or unpleasant memories, like the sight of a telegram messenger who may bring either good or bad news. The most important thing to remember is that the more pleasant or unpleasant the experience the stronger the association of ideas. To most of us a telegram does not do very much but those who have received tragic news by telegram become apprehensive, even terrified, of opening another one. In the same way, those who have received glad tidings by telegram will not be apprehensive of receiving one in the future, knowing quite well that it may not bring good news.

The strongest association is built up by fear. If a child gets bitten by a dog it will be excused for having a lifetime fear of dogs. But if a puppy gets kicked by a child people will wonder why it develops a lifelong fear of children and the breeder will be accused of selling a dog with a bad temperament.

First associations are usually much stronger than subsequent ones. If a child has a very unpleasant experience on the first day at school he or she may take a long time to get over it. If this had not occurred until several weeks at school had passed, it might have had little or no effect. People who show dogs know that if a puppy gets a bad fright at its first show it may dislike shows for life. The same experience a year later might have no effect at all.

Another point worth remembering is that dogs, like us, are much more easily upset and with much more lasting effect when they are off colour. An experience which would have little or no effect under normal circumstances can have disastrous results if it happens when a puppy is teething or has a virus infection, or when a bitch is in season, especially for the first time, and in many cases the animal shows no real symptoms of illness.

For training purposes we try to create the association of ideas which we want in the dog and we do it by correction and reward. This means that we try to make it unpleasant for the dog to do the things we don't want him to do and pleasant for him to do the things we do want. The best example of how we should do this is to be seen by studying a bitch with puppies. First of all she supplies them with food from her own mammary glands and later partly digested food which she regurgitates for them. She also licks and caresses them and makes friendly soft noises which fall somewhere between grunting and whining. The puppies, therefore, associate her with food and caressing and every time they see, hear or smell her they rush joyously to her, just as everyone hopes their new puppy will rush to them; if they feed it, fondle and pet it and make friendly noises to it the chances are that this will happen.

Most people in fact do this, overlooking the fact that the bitch's training does not end there. As the puppies become bigger the bitch, without losing interest in them, does not want to be mauled about by them all the time. Many dog owners put up with that but bitches usually have more sense! So, when the puppies become a bit overbearing the bitch growls at them. Many pups react instinctively to a growl and will stop what they are doing, be it chewing the mother's ear or tail or trying to suckle when there is no milk at the bar, but some bold, dominant pups pay little or no attention. The bitch then repeats her threat and, if there is no response, she will snap at the puppy, often hurting it quite badly human standards. But she does not hurt it often. Next time the puppy hears an angry growl it associates it with a snap and quickly responds. If it does not, it gets another and another until it *does* respond. When a bitch snaps at a puppy it usually gets a fright and runs away a little distance. But it soon crawls back to be licked and caressed and will soon be happy again.

From this I hope you will realise that far from being unnatural, as some people would have use believe, training is the most natural thing in the world, and the bitch with her puppies (many other animals are similar) is an excellent example of simple and straightforward association of ideas. Once upon a time dogs and children were trained according to these simple principles. We have now become more highly educated and use big words like psychiatrist and psychoanalysis – we even have canine psychologists who have never kept a dog in their lives – and everywhere we find disobedient and unhappy dogs and children.

The dog has a simple straightforward mind. He is highly intelligent but less intelligent than we are. If you are less intelligent than your dog just forget about trying to train him! Most of his senses and instincts are far stronger than ours. He sees as well as we do but, because he is nearer the ground and cannot see what we see, many people say his sight is inferior. He hears many times better than we do but from the shouting at many training classes one could believe that all dogs were deaf. His memory is as good if not better than ours, yet people will marvel at their dog recognising them after a six-week holiday. It would be just as logical to be unable to recognise one's own family – and the dog – after that period. Bearing all the above facts in mind let us now try to apply them to the new puppy you have just bought.

To start with remember that he is only a baby suddenly removed from his mother and probably his brothers and sisters too. At this stage he does not want a leader as much as a comforter to replace his mother. Generally speaking

Angela Cavill

women are much better than men at giving confidence to young animals and it is fortunate that in most households it is the woman who takes the new puppy under her wing. This is not just an idea of my own. The Guide Dogs for the Blind Association employs girls to look after the puppies and to do the initial training while men take over the more advanced training when the dog is old enough to need a leader.

You may have noticed when I was talking about creating associations of ideas I said that we *try* to create those we want and avoid those we do not want. But many wrong associations are built up by ignorance or accident. So far as the new puppy is concerned it is more important to avoid wrong associations than to attempt to create ones we want. Remember what I said about first associations and associations which are created when the animal's resilience is low. A young puppy is much more likely to forget an experience whether pleasant or unpleasant than an older one, but any animal is much more likely to get a bad fright in unfamiliar surroundings than in familiar ones.

Many dogs, I believe, have their temperaments completely ruined the first week they go to a new home as a result of the owner's misguided and often cruel attempts to house train them. A human baby is wrapped in nappies and even an older child is excused of wetting its bed if it is worried or upset, for example when he or she has to stay in a strange house. But a canine baby, which probably has never been in a house and which has been taken from its familiar environment by people it has never seen before, is expected to last all night without making a mistake. When it does it has its nose rubbed in it and probably smacked into the bargain. The owner then says 'I can't understand it. When I brought him home he was so friendly and rushed to greet me. Now he runs and hides every time he sees me'. What would you do if someone treated you like that?

Quite apart from the mental and physical suffering caused to the puppy this method has nothing to commend it. It is highly unlikely that the puppy will associate the punishment with the 'crime' which it could not avoid anyhow. There is, however, every likelihood that it will associate the punishment with the person who administers it and/or the place where it occurred. By persisting in this treatment it is possible to turn a normal bold puppy into a complete nervous wreck in less time than you could believe possible. I know dogs do survive this treatment with no apparent ill effects but they have exceptional temperaments in the first place.

The first object therefore should be to get the puppy to like you. And you can't make a dog like you any more than you can a person. All you can do is try to be a likeable person in the eyes of the dog by doing the things he likes. A young puppy likes being cuddled, fondled and petted, but not all the time. He wants to run about and play and chew things up. But you don't want him to chew the house to pieces so give him something to play with. Like all young animals he not only wants but needs to sleep. We all know how lack of sleep frays our nerves, making us irritable and bad tempered, but many puppies are kept continually awake because the owner wants to pet or play with them. Children are allowed, even encouraged to run around chasing a puppy often terrifying the life out of it. They give it no peace and one day they get bitten, which serves them right; but it is the puppy which is put down and the children are given another one to torment. If you can't train your children, it is unlikely you will train a dog. So, save it a lot of suffering by not having it at all.

These are only a few of the many examples of how unpleasant associations can be created by ignorance and lack of consideration. There can still be accidents. Small puppies, especially friendly ones, are adept at getting under one's feet and it is no good saying that it was his own fault that he got trodden on. A puppy does not reason like that and to him you are just an enormous animal towering above him with a huge foot which causes severe pain when plonked on top of him. There are lots of other things which can happen to puppies like doors being slammed on them and furniture falling on top of them, all of which can have a disastrous and sometimes lasting effect.

The best way to avoid unpleasant experiences to the puppy and at the same time save yourself some unpleasant experiences is to provide a play pen. This can be on the lines of a child's play pen and need not be elaborate or expensive. All that is necessary is an enclosure large enough to give a fair amount of freedom and strong enough to prevent the escape of the puppy in question. As there is so much variation in puppies and the conditions applying to different households I shall not attempt to describe the construction of a play pen. The puppy's bed should be placed in the pen. There is a wide variety of beds on the market, such as baskets, ideal for a puppy to chew to pieces. To the puppy an old tea chest or other box on its side is just as good if not better, as it is more enclosed. A board nailed across the front will stop any floor draught and help to keep in an old piece of blanket or other material for bedding. Some newspaper should be spread on the floor of the pen.

The advantage of a play pen should be obvious. While it not only prevents the creation of many undesirable associations of ideas, it also prevents the development of several bad habits. In very few households is there anyone with the time (even if they had the inclination) to keep a constant eye on a puppy. If he is in his pen he cannot mess on the best carpet, chew up the best slippers (they always choose the best ones), get trodden on or jammed in the door. Most important of all he won't get on your nerves or you on his.

If the puppy needs to relieve itself it will use the newspaper which can be picked up without any fuss and bother. Not that I advocate encouraging the puppy to use its play pen as a lavatory! The sooner a puppy is house trained the sooner it is likely to become a pleasant member of the household but there is rarely any need for drastic methods so often advocated. And no correction should be applied until the puppy is happy in its new surroundings and has complete confidence in its new owner. This may take an hour with an exceptionally bold puppy brought up in a house or perhaps two or three days with a less bold puppy reared in a kennel. An eight-week-old puppy should be completely confident in three days, if not there is something wrong either with the pup or the new home. Generally speaking the older a dog is the longer it will take to settle down and the more effect its previous upbringing will have. For instance, a pup reared from eight weeks in a home with children can at six months go to another home with children and settle down right away, but the same pup if reared in a home with a quiet elderly couple, or in kennels with a lot of other dogs, might never get over the shock of a house full of noisy children. We have found that one of the worst ages to change a puppy's environment is between four and five months old when it is teething.

To return to the question of house training few people realise that the average puppy wants to be clean in its own living quarters. All animals born in nests learn at quite an early age to go out of the nest to relieve themselves, thereby keeping their living quarters clean. The object should be to develop this instinct which can usually be done without any correction at all and certainly without the brutal treatment so often administered.

The first essential is an observant owner. Because of its instinct to be clean nearly every puppy will show symptoms of wanting to relieve itself. Unfortunately few owners recognise these symptoms and expect the puppy to ask to go out by whimpering or even barking. The most usual symptom is when the puppy simply starts looking around and probably sniffing the floor. When this happens take him out, wait until he has done what he has to do, praise him well and bring him back in. Don't just push him out and shut the door. He may well have decided that the door mat was the ideal place for his purpose and wait on the door-step until the door opens, when he will come in and do what he intended doing exactly where he intended doing it. If you do catch a puppy actually in the act of squatting down pick him up firmly by the scruff say 'No' or 'Bad boy' in a corrective tone (the equivalent of his mother's growl) and take him out. To a young puppy this is *very* severe correction and should be done quietly without any shouting or flapping of folded newspapers so often recommended.

The important thing is to catch the puppy in the act and this rule applies to all training. Correction after the event (even seconds after) is unlikely to do any good and

more than likely to do a great deal of harm. Remember that we are trying to work on the dog's mind and not his body and he will associate correction with what is on his mind at the time. For instance if a dog is corrected when he is looking at a cat with the obvious intention of chasing it that should be very effective. If he is corrected as he is chasing the cat that should be effective too. But if he chases a cat up a tree and you correct him when he returns to you, you will have corrected him for coming back, not for chasing cats. Thus many dogs are taught by their owners *not* to come back when called – and they still chase cats!

In the same way many puppies become afraid of owners who leave them alone for hours then return and punish them for wetting on the floor – which the poor little blighter could not avoid anyway. 'Of course he knows,' they say. 'Just see how guilty he looks.' But he does not look guilty at all, he simply looks afraid and with very good reason. You can prove this for yourself by scolding any reasonably sensitive dog when it has done nothing wrong and it will immediately look 'guilty' through fear or apprehension.

If one has to leave a puppy for a long period, put him in his play pen and of course he can sleep in it at night. All one has to do then is pick up the soiled newspaper. As he gets older he should learn to wait until he is let out and should be able to do so. A puppy accustomed to newspaper will sometimes prefer to use it in preference to going out. If you take it up and keep an eye on him you should notice when he goes looking for it and take that as a signal to let him out.

Our own dogs are never house trained in the generally accepted sense but simply encouraged to develop their instinct to be clean. Some live in the house and some in kennels and it is rare indeed for an adult to make a mistake in either. They work in studios, live with us in a motor caravan and often stay in hotels and the only problem we ever have is when a director wants a dog to lift its leg in the studio! Having been encouraged to be clean very few of our dogs will do this indoors but will readily oblige outside on the studio lot.

Dog training cannot be divided into compartments and it is useless deciding to spend a fortnight on one exercise and then a fortnight on another. All training must synchronise and a lot of it has to take place simultaneously. There are however, certain 'exercises' which must be learnt before going on to other exercises. These are the basic exercises and the important point about them is that once the teacher and the pupil understand them thoroughly they can go on to more advanced exercises at any time – even after a lapse of several years. Space being limited I intend to deal only with the basic exercises. By the time you have mastered them I hope you will be keen enough on training to buy a book and proceed to more advanced training.

My reason for starting with house training is not because it is more important than other exercise or because it should be taught first. Indeed it is the only exercise which is of no benefit to anyone except the owner – or his friends who visit his house – which is probably why the average owner is so much keener on house training than on teaching the dog not to bite the postman! And that is why I started with it – because it is the first thing most people want to know about. There is actually another reason for starting house training soon after a puppy goes to a new home. A puppy with a strong instinct to be clean will soon choose a secluded spot as a 'loo' and will always go there. If that happens to be at the bottom of the garden it's fine. But if it happens to be behind the piano or the couch in the best room that's not so funny. And if an idea like that (based on an instinct) is allowed to develop it can be very difficult to change. All training must endeavour to create good habits and prevent bad ones.

One good habit which the puppy should learn right from the start is to come when called. In spite of everything you believe or have been told about dogs that 'understand every word said to him' dogs do not in fact, understand any words at all. They simply recognise sounds (far more accurately than we do) and they associate these sounds with certain actions. If your dog gets excited when you mention 'Walk' it is simply because he associates that sound (not a word to him) with going for a walk. Instead of recognising that simple fact dog owners resort to spelling the word. Very soon the dog associates the sounds W-A-L-K with going for a walk and his owners think he has learnt to spell!

At this stage we are mainly concerned with encouraging the puppy to come to us in response to a particular sound. The sound is usually the dog's name and where there are a lot of dogs, such as we keep, it is important that each and every one responds to its own name and to no other. But we do not go around repeating a dog's name over and over again for no reason at all. We use the dog's name when we want him to come to us – and if we don't want him we don't call him. The average owner, however, appears unable to desist from repeating the puppy's name every time he sees it. Not only that – the whole family, friends and neighbours will want to have cosy chats with any new puppy repeating its name over and over again in the process. Any new puppy we get will come to us in response to its name within a day or two but the average puppy hears its name so much that it completely ignores the sound just as it does the sound of the radio or television.

Constantly repeated sounds without association become ignored. For that reason it is often advisable to teach a dog to come to you in response to a different sound altogether like 'here' or 'come'. The word matters not and it is just as easy to teach a dog to come by saying 'go' as by saying 'come'. What does matter is that you always use the same command and use it in the right tone of voice. As I said earlier, a puppy instinctively cowers or even runs away at the sound of its mother's growl and will rush to greet her when she makes her soft welcoming noise, which is almost inaudible to human ears. The ability to change the tone of voice is vital in training and is one of the gifts which divides successful trainers into successful and unsuccessful. Don't confuse tone with volume. It is never necessary to shout at a puppy in the confines of its own house.

Now we come to the big question. How do you teach this charming puppy to rush to you in joyous bounds every time you call it? To start with you want to persuade rather than try to make it come. Later you may have to make him (he may have lost some of his charm by then!) but try persuasion first.

Obviously you should start by calling the puppy in a nice friendly persuasive tone of voice, never in a harsh correcting tone. If you stand straight up he is likely to stand back staring at the great thing towering above him but if you squat down he should come up to you even if you do not ask him.

A timid puppy will move away every time you move towards him but is almost certain to come nearer if you move away from him.

An outstretched hand with moving fingers will attract nearly any puppy, and many adult dogs, while the same hand with fist clenched will be ignored. There is a general belief that one should always present the back of the hand to a strange dog. Working with dogs as I do in close contact with a great variety of self-styled dog lovers I find the efforts to carry out this exercise as amusing as it is unsuccessful.

Perhaps the commonest of all mistakes which people make in approaching a strange dog (and that includes a new puppy) is to stare at it. The only animal which likes its friends to look it 'straight in the eye' is the human being. Other animals do this only if they are afraid of each other or are about to attack. Watch two dogs meeting. If they look straight at each other you can expect a fight but if they approach shoulder to shoulder and walk stiffly round and round each other they will end up on friendly terms; so never stare at a new puppy when you are trying to get on friendly terms.

Now you are out in the garden with your pride and joy and you want him to come when called. He is probably sniffing around the gatepost or digging up the flower bed. Don't call him – for the simple and obvious reason that he won't come anyhow! An untrained puppy will do the thing which provides, or is likely to provide, the greatest pleasure at the time. Anyone who thinks that his voice is more attractive to a puppy than a hole in the ground or a smell on a gatepost has got the puppy's priorities wrong. Wait until the puppy appears to have nothing important to do and call it then. The best time is usually when he happens to be coming to you anyhow. Crouch down, hand extended, and call the puppy in a friendly persuasive tone. When he reaches you make a great fuss, fondle him and possibly offer a reward in the form of food. Do this several times when the puppy is sure to come and he will soon associate the sound of his name with the reward of food and/or petting. He will then have this association of ideas to strengthen the natural inclination to go to a friendly voice or hand. In most cases this combination will soon be strong enough to induce the puppy to leave the hole he is digging or the smell he is sniffing.

The mistakes most people make is in never calling the puppy unless he is doing something they don't want him to do – which is usually something he *does* want to do. Every time you call a puppy and he obeys you (even if he happened to be coming anyhow) you have gone a step forward. Every time you call him and he disobeys you you have gone a step back. And if you persist in calling him when he is certain to disobey you, you will actually teach him *not* to come when called. Whatever you do, never, under any circumstances, scold or correct a dog in any way when it comes to you – no matter how much you feel like murdering it!

Now we have a puppy which comes to you in response to reward alone. But he will only do so if the reward is better than the alternative – and dog's lives, like ours, are made up of alternatives. A puppy will probably find food and petting more rewarding than aimlessly digging a hole or sniffing round a gatepost. But if the hole leads to a stinking old bone previously buried there or, when the dog is a bit older, a bitch in season has been around the gatepost, cooing voice, outstretched hand and pocketfuls of titbits may prove to be a poor alternative. We must then resort to correction as well as reward to build up the association we want. It should be noted that correction is only resorted to when reward has failed.

Our puppy is back in the same hole and you call him as before. But this is a much more interesting hole and, if the puppy responds at all, it is merely to look up as if saying 'Hang on a minute, I'm busy'. Here we have a situation where it is very easy to correct the puppy as he is doing the wrong thing and you should always take advantage of such opportunities. You have *asked* the puppy to come by calling his name in a nice friendly tone and he has refused. Call his name again, this time *telling* him to come in a very firm tone. It is possible that the puppy may respond to this change of tone. If so, change your tone of voice and whole attitude completely, and reward him with enthusiasm. If he does not respond pick up a handful of earth or small gravel and call him again even more harshly. If he does not respond this time throw the earth or gravel at him. As this 'hail' descends on him from heaven he will almost certainly get a fright and look round for a protector – that's you! Call him to you, make a great fuss of him and do all you can to console him in his misfortune. The object is to get him to associate the harsh tone of voice with something nasty out of the blue. He must not know that you threw it and, if you do it properly, it is almost certain that next time he hears that harsh tone he will anticipate another 'hailstorm' and rush to you for protection – which you must always provide.

Never allow a puppy to run loose in a strange place until he will come to you every time you call him in the house or garden. Even then, you may find that when he sees another dog in the park he rushes off. I cannot over-emphasise the importance of nipping this habit in the bud and the best way for the novice is probably by using a check cord –

about thirty feet of light cord attached to a dog's collar at one end with the other end in your hand. Let the puppy rush off and, as he nears the end of the cord call his name in a harsh tone. This time, instead of the handful of earth, the jerk on the check cord will provide the correction. He will probably do a somersault but don't worry. This method has been used by generations of gun dog trainers and I have never heard of a dog hurting himself. As he recovers from the jerk call him in a nice friendly tone and, when he reaches you, reward him lavishly. Never drag him to you. The line should be used as a means of correction when the dog tries to run away but you should encourage him to you by reward.

This method of training should naturally never be carried out until the dog is on a collar and lead and it is unlikely that a puppy will run after other dogs until he is about six months old. He will have to learn to go on a collar and lead before you take him out in public, and the place to teach him is not on the street or in the park but in his own garden or even indoors. Remember that a lead should never be regarded as a means of making a dog go with you but merely as a means of preventing him going too far away. Never put a collar and lead on a puppy until he will follow you without one.

There is a lot of argument about the best type of collar. Generally speaking, an ordinary buckled leather collar is as good as any for a puppy to start with. The puppy can be allowed to wear one and become quite familiar with it before the lead is put on. Start with a long lead and use it only to stop the puppy. Encourage him to come with you by rewarding him in the ways I have already described. Providing he will follow you without a lead (even if you do carry food in your pocket) he should soon follow you with one. It is more a question of familiarisation than actual training.

The usual problem is not how to get a puppy to go on a lead but how to stop him pulling once he has become familiar with it.

Here again this should be stopped before it becomes a habit, which is easier to prevent than to cure. It is important that when the puppy pulls you do not pull against him. Correct him for pulling with a sharp jerk on the lead and when he comes back to you in response, praise him well. Obviously you cannot jerk a dog on a short lead. For training a lead should be three or four feet long, pliable (we now use nylon web leads almost entirely), with a strong clip. If the puppy pulls, let the lead go suddenly and, before he has regained his balance, give him a sharp jerk. With a young puppy quite a small jerk will suffice, but it requires a considerable amount of skill and strength to cure an adult dog of pulling. There is little pleasure in taking out a dog which constantly pulls so, for your own sake as well as the dog's, don't let the habit develop.

If, in spite of your efforts, the puppy is pulling by the time he is six months old I would suggest taking him to a local training class. I have mixed feelings about training classes where one often finds the blind leading the blind – not very successfully either! I get a great many cries for help from dog owners and almost all of them have already attended training classes! Some of the advice given by self-styled experts is quite frightening. I have met many sensitive dogs with temperaments completely ruined by classes.

On the other hand I know many dogs and owners who have benefited beyond belief. Like many other successful trainers, I started by going to classes. It really all depends on the instructor who in this country (not in America) gives his services free. Unfortunately free advice is often worth just what it costs. My advice is to go along to a training class (the Kennel Club will give you a list of those in your area) without your dog and see whether dogs which have been attending for some time behave in the way you want your dog to behave.

You now have a puppy which is clean in the house, comes when you call it (and stays with you) and walks on a loose lead. The other important exercise to make him a pleasure rather than a nuisance is that he stays where he is told without bringing complaints from the neighbours. Here we must go right back to the beginning with the puppy in the play pen. If, when you leave him, he cries to

get out and you take him out you will be rewarding him for crying. It is incredible how quickly a young puppy will learn that whenever it wants attention all it has to do is howl. The longer you stay with a puppy coddling and consoling him the longer he will whine or howl when you leave him. If you go away and leave him alone he will probably howl for a bit and then settle down and go to sleep. A puppy accustomed from the start to being left alone in his play pen is unlikely to create any problems when you come to leave him in the car or any other strange place.

If he does persist in howling or barking when left alone, put him in his pen or just shut him in a room and go away. Stop when you get out of sight and wait for the noise to start. When it does, go back quietly. The puppy won't hear you when he is making a noise but he will whenever he stops, so you must stop and wait until he starts again. The idea is to get right up to the door while he is actually making a noise, then open it suddenly (which will surprise him anyhow) grab hold of him and scold him severely. Now start all over again, and if he makes a noise repeat the whole process. It is unlikely that he will make a noise this time so wait a few moments (don't tempt Providence by waiting too long) and go back to him again. This time make a great fuss to reward him for being quiet.

The usual mistake people make is unintentionally rewarding the dog for making a noise. They say 'Now, now, be a good boy. Don't make a noise', or 'It's all right, Mummy's here. No need to cry about it', and they say it all in the most soothing and rewarding tone possible. Having been rewarded by tone of voice (probably by gentle stroking too) for barking or whining the dog naturally does it again, and again, and again for as long as he is rewarded. It is interesting to note that bad tempered owners never have problems of this sort. They don't wonder what to do or read books on the subject. The dog irritates them by making a noise and, as it is actually barking, is told in no uncertain terms to 'Shut up'. If it doesn't, it gets a hefty clout on the ear and next time it hears 'Shut up' it shuts up! That is not how I train dogs or believe that dogs should be trained but it is effective.

Your pup should now be clean in the house, come when called (at any time and in any place) and be quiet when left on his own. And that is more than can be said for many of the dogs working in the Obedience Championships at Crufts! If you do aspire to more advanced training (and I hope some of my readers will) there are several books on the subject and plenty of people willing to offer advice.

JOHN HOLMES

An animal man if ever there was one, John Holmes was born and brought up on a farm in Scotland, and is the son of a famous breeder and exhibitor of Clydesdale horses and a judge of horses and cattle. As a boy he kept terriers who earned their keep by keeping the farm free of vermin. As an encore the terrier team entertained the farm workers and locals with a variety of party tricks. Later he graduated to training sheep- and cattle-dogs, using them for real work; he drove sheep ten miles to Perth market once a week, summer and winter, for a number of years.

He bought his first Corgi, Nippy of Drumharrow, in 1933 for two guineas, and later owned many famous Corgis. Mr Holmes took up obedience training after the war and in 1950 won the Junior Stakes at the ASPADS Trials; he then started training difficult and disobedient dogs for other people, and in no time at all became a prominent figure with a nationwide reputation.

In his own words, at this point he really began to learn about dogs and, more important, dog people. He ran dog training classes at Henley on Thames, and among other successes the instructor married his 'star pupil'. Together, Mr and Mrs Holmes built up a team of dogs who gave displays all over the British Isles – a mongrel from the team started his film career in 'Knave of Hearts'. This was quickly followed by a television series of dog programmes, 'Your Dog and Mine', for which John supplied the performers. Since then he has handled all sorts of other animals, including rats, on hundreds of films, television plays and commercials, and has appeared in numerous documentaries and discussion programmes on television. His film, 'A Tale of Two Puppies', was networked over all regions around Christmas 1970, and he has also made a seven-episode series for Southern Television called 'Training the Family Dog' based on his book *The Family Dog* (now in its fifth edition). Other books by John Holmes include *The Farmer's Dog* (about training sheep- and cattle-dogs) and *Obedience Training for Dogs*.

J.C.

7 The Cocker Spaniel in the Field

BY JOYCE CADDY

Cocker Spaniels are popular companions for people who like a day's shooting, whether over driven game or on a rough shoot; the dogs too enjoy their days out. The quality of their work, however, depends on many things, one of which is the basic training they have been given. For the man doing rough shooting, the standard will probably not need to be so high as that demanded of a dog running in a field trial—it all depends on what the owner expects of his dog.

Basically, a Cocker should be under control when off the lead, respond quickly to commands from his handler, and be agreeable (i.e. not aggressive in any way) to other dogs working on the shoot. He should also show that he is not gunshy, and that he will face tough cover (i.e. bramble, rough undergrowth, bracken, nettles, etc.) when hunting for game to flush out and when retrieving shot game. In addition to all this, a Cocker must prove that he is capable of retrieving to his handler, and he must carry the bird tenderly, without damaging it.

There are various forms of competition for Cockers in the field, the highest standard of all being required at a Field Trial. This is a competition run under Kennel Club regulations, with a maximum of sixteen dogs competing. (If more than that number are entered, a draw takes place to see which dogs will be fortunate enough to take part.) There are two judges, and the dogs are numbered; the judges work in line with each other, judge 'A' taking the odd numbers, while judge 'B' takes the evens. On the outside of each of the judges is an official 'gun'. It depends very much on the terrain as to how far distant the two dogs and their handlers are from each other, but they must be sufficiently far apart not to interfere with each other's work. When a judge is satisfied with the work of a particular Spaniel, he will ask his steward for another dog, and so on through the list. When all have been run once, judge 'A' will then take the even numbers and judge 'B' the odd, thus ensuring that both judges have seen all the dogs working. At the end of the second round, the judges

compare notes and make the awards as decided. Should they feel that there is little between two or more dogs, they are at liberty to call for a 'run off' if they wish to compare them.

The basic requirements are that the Spaniel should at all times work within range, with good ground treatment; under no circumstances should it pass over game on the beat it is working—the first job of a Spaniel is to find game and flush within range of the gun. The direction of the wind can have a considerable influence on the way a dog will work the ground. With a head-on wind, the dog will probably quarter the ground systematically left to right, and *vice versa*, checking all likely game-holding cover (i.e. brambles, nettles), but keeping within gunshot distance of his handler. With a following wind it may be very different in its approach and may start well ahead of, and work back towards his handler. During this period, the judge can assess the game-finding ability and scenting power of the dog, as well as his pace, drive and treatment of ground. If a dog 'points' or hesitates momentarily before flushing game, this is regarded as an added refinement, but the dog must flush on the command of his handler. A dog should 'stop' when flushing has been carried out, and when the

Sally Anne Thompson

bird has been shot, but he is allowed to move a little in order to mark where the bird falls, if his vision is otherwise obscured. He must not make any attempt to retrieve until the command to do so is given.

When the command to retrieve is given, the dog should pick it up cleanly, return quickly and deliver it to the hand of his handler. Should the cover be very rough, the dog may not be able to return quickly, particularly if carrying a heavy burden (e.g. a cock pheasant or a large hare), but he should return steadily and not put down his burden until he gets to his handler. The judges will examine all the game retrieved for signs of 'hard mouth'; this means that the dog should not have damaged the bird in any way —no crushed bones, etc.

When working, a Cocker should have drive and thrust, face cover well, and at the same time be amenable and gay. Given all these qualities, a Cocker working well is a joy to watch.

Another type of competition which is run by many Spaniel Clubs is called a 'Working' or 'Cold Game' Test. This is run on similar lines to a Field Trial, but the dogs are not required to hunt for live game—they are expected to find a hidden 'dummy' or cold bird, and retrieve this to

their handlers. Various grades of Cold Game Tests are run, from the beginners' stage to that of the experienced dogs. These tests are extremely useful in maintaining the natural instinct and ability of Spaniels to work, even though their owners may not have the facilities or the time to train and work their dogs up to Field Trial standards.

When dogs have entered and won three Championship Field Trial Open Stakes they are able to be described as Field Trial Champion (often abbreviated to F.T.Ch.). There is another title of 'Champion' which is used to describe a dog which has won three Challenge Certificates (or more) in the show ring, and has also proved his ability as a working dog, having been tested by two Field Trial judges under Field Trial conditions—but not in competition with other dogs—for what is described as a Qualifying Certificate. Without this certificate, or proof of his having retained his natural instinct, any dog which wins three or more Challenge Certificates in the show ring can only be called a Show Champion.

Whether a Cocker Spaniel is kept purely as a pet, or household companion, or as a shooting companion, he will always enjoy his 'work'—whether this be retrieving a ball or stick in the garden, or a full day's work in the fields.

8

Showing; Starting a Kennel

BY KAY DOXFORD

I have seen many beginners plunging into championship show competition at their first attempt in the show ring, and being desperately disappointed that they have had no wins. This is *not* the way to start. Begin by going to the shows without a dog and watch around the Cocker ring; see how the dogs are presented and how they are shown— in other words, learn the drill. Make your first plunge at a local sanction show. Having gained some confidence, enter at the open shows, and after a spell of that you should be ready to start entering in a few minor classes at a championship show. Most of the established breeders are very helpful, and they are usually only too pleased to make an appointment for a visit to their kennels.

Learn all you can about presentation. The trimming of the Cocker Spaniel is very much of an art (see chapter 3) and the finished product must look as natural as possible. I deplore the 'barbering' of the coats which unfortunately can sometimes be seen. I know it's quicker, but the good coat which can be achieved with care and constant attention does look so lovely that trimming by hand repays one a hundred times over.

I know it is the wish of many a newcomer to become a breeder of show stock, and many visualise themselves gaining top honours in a very short time. Believe me, one has to be prepared for many years of hard work before the coveted challenge certificate comes one's way. Occasionally, of course, a beginner has the good fortune to acquire a top winner at the first time of asking, but as a rule there is no short cut to successful breeding—it is mostly a process of trial and error.

Of one thing I am certain, and that is that the new breeder must start by buying a puppy or adult from a knowledgeable breeder who has been producing sound, consistent winners over a number of years. You really cannot hope to breed anything of outstanding merit if you take a pet bitch of perhaps rather hotch-potch breeding to a leading stud dog—he can't do everything, and the influence of the dam is often dominant. If you

possess a very well-bred pet bitch bought from a good breeder, well, that's a different matter. Ask the breeder's advice as regards a mating for her, and you might well strike lucky in founding a nice line of Cockers.

There are many Cocker clubs throughout the country, and these always welcome newcomers to the breed, being only too happy to give both encouragement and advice when needed, for the members have the good of the Cocker very much at heart. (Names of such clubs can be obtained from the Kennel Club.) Several of the clubs hold social gatherings, matches and handling classes, as well as varying types of shows. By chatting with other breeders and owners you will really begin to pick up tips and learn much about the merry little Cocker.

I would advise anyone on the brink of starting up in Cockers to decide on the colour in which to specialise. There are so many to choose from that a visit to a breed championship show or a look round a kennel that handles both 'solids' and parti-colours can be of enormous help before you make your final decision. Then go to the kennel of your choice and talk to the owner. Remember that because Cocker puppies are extremely popular, many kennels have bookings on expected litters, so don't be too impatient. Get on the list and then ask the owner to advise you on a promising youngster. It will pay dividends, I feel sure. The same applies when booking a stud dog for a bitch; the big winners and the dogs who consistently sire winners are always heavily booked up, and it only leads to disappointment if you leave a booking too late.

There is no need to keep a very large kennel to breed really good stock. It is much better to aim at quality rather than quantity.

Cockers are a sturdy, healthy breed and make both excellent whelpers and mothers, so if stock is purchased from a kennel that breeds for good looks and, above all, for temperament, the dogs can give their owners many happy and rewarding years. There is nothing as exciting as breeding 'a really good one', and gaining top honours, and nothing as worthwhile as building up a kennel of typical, healthy stock that wins in good competition, and also gives

pleasure to the pet-owner, and if required, satisfaction as a working dog. Brains and beauty *can* go together in the typical Cocker, and it is for this reason, I think, that our breed still remains so very popular both at shows and with the general public.

Exporting
This now assumes a major rôle in most well-known kennels, and many very good Cocker adults and puppies leave these shores for every country imaginable. Before exporting, however, one should make very thorough enquiries regarding any request for stock. Be sure to find out just what type of Cocker is preferred in the country in question. Some countries like dogs on the small side, some prefer them to be larger. When judging the breed in many places abroad I have often noticed how different countries vary in the assessment of points in their Cocker judging. I always feel that it is best to send puppies which are on the small side to the warmer countries, as they seem to 'grow on' in hot climates, whereas the larger puppy is the better bet for a colder clime, as it will not tend to finish up too big, as

might be the case if it went to a hot country. Again, if you have an adult dog that plainly dislikes hot weather, don't accept any offer for him that would take him to a hot climate—it would only cause disappointment to the new owners and make the dog unhappy. These are the kind of animals to send to the Scandinavian countries, where they can enjoy life to the full and bring much pleasure to their owners.

Overseas breeders are in the main very keen and intelligent, and I do impress on anyone who has an order for an overseas buyer to send only the best; after all, once the animal has been sent it cannot be returned, as it could be if sold in this country.

The standard of the breed is very high in most countries, as I have seen when privileged to stay in the homes of several of my clients overseas. This was a most rewarding experience, as I was really able to see behind the scenes in their kennels and to realise how much care and hard work they give to their dogs.

9

Breeding

BY BETTY PENN-BULL

There is an old theory that every bitch should have a litter, but there seems to be no evidence to support this, so unless there is a definite desire to breed, the certainty of placing the resulting puppies satisfactorily, and the ability to provide the necessary care and attention, it is not advisable to embark on mating a bitch.

My opinion is that a bitch is best bred from either regularly or not at all, and that the single, so-called 'therapeutic' litter may well unsettle her, awakening the maternal and breeding instincts which are then subsequently thwarted if she is not allowed further puppies.

I have known many maiden bitches which have lived healthy lives into ripe old age, and I do not advise anyone to mate a bitch unless the puppies are really wanted. Never do so 'for her sake' and risk bringing puppies into the world for which it may be impossible to find good and suitable homes.

There are new opinions these days in regard to spaying bitches, and this now seems to be more acceptable than it used to be. But it is important that a bitch is fully developed before this is done, and she should have had at least one season in order to have reached complete maturity. Guide Dogs For The Blind use spayed bitches almost without exception, and this has not been found to affect their disposition, health, well-being or ability to work adversely.

Small breeds are usually easily controlled when in season, but with the larger ones, or where premises are not completely secure from invasion by trespassing dogs, spaying is certainly preferable to mis-mating and a subsequent unwanted litter.

Bitches used for breeding should conform to certain standards physically and mentally, and those falling short of these requirements should be discarded. They should be sound and healthy, of good type and conformation, and free from structural, organic or hereditary defects. In addition they should be of good temperament; nervous or bad-

tempered stock should not be bred from. People sometimes
appear to have the wrong ideas about breeding and I have
heard remarks like, 'She is so nervous and excitable, I
think a litter will steady her'; 'She keeps getting skin
trouble, I hope having puppies will help to clear it up'. I
feel this argument should be in reverse. Are these dogs
suitable to be bred from? Do we want half a dozen more
with poor temperaments or with some physical disability?
If the answer is that we do not, then the simple solution is
not to breed from such stock, and they should be excluded
from one's breeding programme. The possibility of benefit-
ing the parent at the expense of the unborn young is a
wrong concept.

Before being mated the bitch should be in top condition
and perfect health. She should be well nourished on a
properly balanced diet with ample protein, but it is preferable if she is a little on the lean side rather than slightly
too fat.

Bitches normally come into season for the first time at
about nine months of age, and thereafter at six monthly
intervals. But there may be some variation in these times
and this is not necessarily an indication of any abnormality. Small dogs in particular may have their first heat
as young as seven or eight months of age, while larger
ones may be a year old or even older. The cycle may vary
too, and occasionally a bitch will go twelve months between
seasons, while with some of the smaller breeds it may
occur again after only four months' intervals. But if a
bitch has three seasons in a year, one of these will not be
fertile. Usually, after a litter the cycle adjusts and the times
revert to the normal six months. When a bitch is due in
season she should be tested each day with a swab of cotton
wool pressed to the vulva to check for the first sign of
colour. She can then be observed, and the pattern of her
season noted.

As a rule, dogs tend to sniff around a bitch and show
interest before the season actually starts, and this is often
an indication that it is pending. But once the colour
appears most dogs leave a bitch severely alone during the

early period and I do not usually find it necessary to segregate her for at least six or seven days. After this time she must be carefully isolated.

Colour usually continues for about nine or ten days and then it gradually begins to fade, and by about twelve days, which is normally the height of the season, there is either just a pinkish tinge or it is practically colourless. As a rule the heat lasts for three weeks and the bitch must be kept isolated until the end of this period whether mated or not.

With some of the smaller breeds there is a more rapid cycle, the colour fades sooner and the bitch may be ready at eight or nine days, and the season completely over in fourteen or fifteen days. Some of the larger breeds may not be ready to mate until fourteen to sixteen days or even later, and their season may last twenty-four days, or occasionally even longer, so each bitch must be studied individually. It is important to note details of the first season as this can be helpful on subsequent occasions if a mating is intended.

With the smaller breeds the second season is a suitable time for mating, and this usually occurs at about fifteen months of age. But if a bitch is being shown, or it is not convenient, she can be left until later. It is advisable when possible to have her first litter by about three years of age while the frame is still elastic and has not hardened too much.

If a bitch is bred from regularly but has not been over-bred, I have known a number to continue having successful litters up to eight years of age. But it is important that she is maintained in good condition and receives the right care and attention.

It is not possible to generalise in regard to the frequency with which one can mate a bitch as each case must be assessed on its own merits.

As a rough guide the larger breeds which also tend to have larger litters may need a longer time between litters. With the smaller breeds one can often have two litters in succession and then miss a season without putting an undue strain on the bitch. But other factors come into account too, particularly the number of puppies produced and reared. If a bitch had seven or eight and reared all I would rest her a year before the next litter. But if she had only three or four I would consider mating her at her next heat. This would apply during the prime of her life, between two and six years old, but after six years of age I would not breed from her more than once a year.

Other factors must be considered too, such as her general health, condition and activity and whether she is an easy whelper. Some dogs of seven are like four-year-olds, and others are like ten-year-olds, so all these matters must be taken into account.

Arrangements should be made well in advance with the owner of the selected stud dog, and it is customary for her to visit him. A provisional date should be fixed as soon as she starts in season which can be varied later if necessary.

If the bitch is sent by rail she should be despatched two or three days before the height of her season and in consultation with the owner of the dog. She should be sent in a secure and comfortable box, properly labelled and with careful arrangements for her collection.

If she is taken personally which is preferable whenever possible, it is important the timing is correct to ensure maximum prospects of a successful outcome, and this entails the careful assessment of the vital factors of the timing, colour and her reactions. On arrival the bitch should be allowed a free run to relieve herself, to stretch her legs and to settle down a little after her journey, before being introduced to the dog. The actual mating procedure is dealt with under the section concerned with the stud dog.

After mating, the bitch must be kept segregated until the completion of her season, and she can then resume her normal life.

Care of the Bitch In Whelp
The bitch in whelp should be well cared for, but not coddled. For the first few weeks she may carry on with her ordinary routine providing this does not entail any excessive exertion. But she will be all the better for plenty of freedom

and exercise, interspersed with adequate rest periods. She should not be allowed to get cold or wet, and should also be protected from excessive heat.

During the last few weeks several short walks are preferable to one long one, but she should be encouraged to keep active with gentle exercise until the end, although avoiding anything unduly strenuous. She should have as much liberty as possible and should not be closely confined except for minimal periods.

Feeding the in-whelp bitch may vary to some degree. With the small breeds, and with some which are not always easy whelpers, great care must be taken not to over-feed, and the aim is to produce small, strong puppies at birth, as larger ones may well be the cause of trouble at whelping time.

I feed as usual for the first six weeks, but I do ensure there is an ample meat ration, plus a limited amount of biscuit and raw or cooked vegetables. I give two equal meals for the last three weeks, increasing the meat allowance but decreasing the starch to a minimum. I give cod liver oil daily, but this is the only additive my bitches in whelp receive as they are a breed which are not always easy whelpers, so I ration them carefully. I do not add calcium or bone meal, or give milk or eggs or other extras.

But with many other breeds, and particularly the larger ones, it will be advisable to step up the rations after mating, and probably to provide various additives too, as this particular problem of whelping does not apply in all cases.

The big breeds usually have larger litters and the puppies are proportionately smaller at birth in relation to the size of the dam. So within certain limits the breeder must be guided by the needs of the individual bitch in deciding on the correct policy.

I give a small teaspoonful of liquid paraffin daily during the last week. I also give the bitch a thorough grooming and overhaul several days before the litter is due. This consists of a good brushing and combing into every corner. She is then sponged over with a cloth wrung out in weak Dettol and warm water, paying particular attention to the feet, under the body, the head, between the legs and under the tail. The anal gland is checked and cleared if necessary. The eyes and ears are examined and treated if required, and the mouth and teeth are inspected and cleaned if necessary.

Any excessive hair round feet, tummy and other parts may be tidied up if desired, but although I have a breed with furnishings I do not remove them from my bitches. Some breeders do, and this is a matter for the individual to decide.

The Whelping Quarters

The bitch should be introduced to the place where she is to whelp some days before the event, so she feels settled and relaxed there. This should be a quiet room or building, or an enclosed pen where she has privacy and is not worried by other dogs or by children or strangers.

The whelping box should be placed here, and it should be roomy enough for her to lie full length and still allow a margin of space beyond this. It should be raised on low slats to allow air to circulate beneath the base. There should be a removable board to slot into the front, but this should be taken out before whelping to avoid any risk of injury when the bitch goes in and out of the box. The sides of the box should be high enough to protect the bitch and puppies from draughts and a removable lid is an advantage.

A crush barrier should be provided which can be inserted into the box, with a clearance of two or more inches from the ground, and two or more inches from the sides of the box, according to the size of the dog, to avoid the possibility of the puppies being pressed behind the dam, and perhaps suffocated. This is similar to the pig-rail used for farrowing sows and provides a safe alley-way while the puppies are small. This barrier should not be put into position until after the bitch has finished whelping and it can be removed when the puppies are two or three weeks old, when they require more room and will be stronger.

I use an infra-red lamp for my litters and this is positioned across one corner of the box, so there is a warm spot for the puppies, but the opposite corner is cool if the dam prefers to lie there.

My whelping box has vinyl on the floor and this is then covered with several layers of newspaper and finally a thick blanket for the bitch and litter.

The Whelping

Bitches carry their young for sixty-three days, but this is subject to some variation. It is quite usual for a bitch to whelp three days early, while some of the smaller breeds may have their puppies five days before time. Puppies born more than five days early have a limited chance of survival. Some bitches may go overtime, but if this extends more than two or three days there is some cause for concern and there may be trouble ahead.

The first indication that whelping may be imminent is a drop in temperature which will fall below 100° (normal temperature in the dog is 101·4°). This may occur two or three days before the actual whelping, but when the temperature drops to 98° or 97° the whelping will generally occur within twenty-four hours.

The preliminary signs are restlessness, trembling, yawning, panting, bed-making, and possibly vomiting. Food is usually refused, and there is often a desire to pass water frequently.

All these symptoms may be present, or only some, and they may last for some hours, or even intermittently for a full day or more. But the whelping as such does not really commence until the contractions begin, so until that time it is a matter of waiting for further developments.

If there is a rise in temperature or a black or green discharge, trouble is indicated and veterinary advice must be sought without delay.

But if all appears normal do not interfere unnecessarily, but allow the bitch the opportunity to whelp. Some are slower than others, and it sometimes pays to be patient providing there are no abnormal symptoms.

Many bitches like the comfort of their owner's presence at this time, and a reassuring word and a little fondling will encourage them. Firm, but gentle stroking down the back is sometimes helpful in stimulating the contractions.

The bitch should not be fussed or agitated and the owner

should remain calm and cheerful. The bitch can be offered glucose and milk or glucose and water from time to time, or she may be given a little brandy or whisky, but she should not have any solid food during whelping as this may cause vomiting.

The first puppy may appear quite quickly once the contractions start, or it may not come for two or three hours, or even more in some cases, as some bitches are much slower than others.

It is sometimes difficult to decide at what stage assistance should be given, and if an owner is a complete novice it is helpful to have an experienced breeder available who can advise in the event of any queries or difficulties or suggest when professional help is necessary.

The puppy should arrive head first, contained in its sac and with the afterbirth attached, and the dam should quickly release the puppy, cleaning it thoroughly and eating the afterbirth. But some bitches, particularly maidens, are slow at freeing the puppy's head, and in this case the breeder must do so without delay or fluid will get into the puppy's lungs and this may be fatal. The bitch should then be encouraged to lick and massage the puppy. If it is slow in breathing it should be rubbed and shaken and any fluid drawn from the nose and mouth; warmth is very important in helping to revive it.

The flat-nosed breeds are not usually able to attend to their newly-born whelps, and the attendant must be prepared to assist them by removing the puppy from the bag and severing the cord. The puppy should then be offered to the dam for her to clean and lick. If several puppies are born in rapid succession it may be advisable to remove some of the earlier ones temporarily and place them in a warm box away from the dam until the whelping is completed so that the newer arrivals can receive more attention, and the earlier ones do not get cold and neglected. But if this upsets the dam they must be left with her and endeavours made to keep them warm and dry. I use thick newspapers for the whelping and old sacks or blankets, and I put in more paper or old towels as we go along, to try and keep the bed as clean and dry as possible.

When the whelping is finished one person should take the bitch out to make herself comfortable. Meanwhile, a second person should gently lift out the puppies, then remove the soiled bedding, wipe round the box and put in fresh paper and a clean blanket. The anti-crush frame should then be inserted, the front board slotted in and the puppies replaced. The dam should then be allowed back, to find everything ship-shape, thus avoiding her being agitated by a lot of commotion going on around her.

She should be offered a warm drink and then left quietly to rest for a few hours, although it is generally wise to keep an unobtrusive eye on her to make sure all is well. I leave a small light for the first few days as I prefer a dull emitter lamp over the bed.

Post-Natal Care and Feeding
For the first few days after whelping it is important to check the bitch's mammary glands regularly. Run the hands lightly over all her teats and these should be soft and yielding. If one or more are hard and congested this indicates the puppies are not suckling from these, and this may result in milk fever or an abcess, so steps must be taken immediately to alleviate the condition.

The trouble is more likely to occur with small litters when the puppies are obtaining adequate milk supplies without drawing on all the teats. Those most likely to be affected are the back ones which often carry heavy milk yields, and to a lesser extent the front ones may also be affected. The middle breasts do not seem as likely to be involved and are usually those most readily drawn on by the puppies.

As soon as the condition is diagnosed the affected breast should be gently massaged and softened with warm poultices to ease the pressure. Then some of the milk should be drawn off, and when it is flowing freely one of the strongest puppies should be placed on the teat and encouraged to suck. When he has had his fill he should be replaced by another until the breast is clear.

There may be no further trouble once it is soft and pliable, and the puppies may now use it normally. But it must be watched and the treatment repeated if necessary. Once a gland becomes really congested and hard the puppies will avoid it as they are unable to draw the milk from it in this condition, so it is essential to get the milk flowing to avert any possible complications. The dam must also be kept under careful observation to ensure there are no complications as an aftermath of the whelping. Any rise in temperature, refusal of food, vomiting, unhealthy discharge, or diarrhoea should alert the breeder.

There may be retention of a puppy and if this is dead professional help must be summoned without delay; or perhaps the bitch has failed to pass one or more of the afterbirths, in which case an injection to encourage this may be called for, or antibiotics may be necessary. So it is essential to seek advice immediately if any abnormal symptoms such as these should occur.

If there is no infection and no complications, the bitch will usually be happy and relaxed after the birth, and ready to take nourishment, so any signs of discomfort or distress should cause the breeder to suspect something to be wrong, and he should therefore take the necessary steps to obtain advice or help should any untoward symptoms manifest themselves.

Once the puppies are safely born the bitch should be fed

generously and this applies to nursing mothers of all breeds as suckling puppies imposes a great strain on the dam.

I give fluid feeds only for the first twenty-four hours. Then for the next twenty-four hours I add semi-solids such as fish, minced meat and eggs. If all is going normally I then gradually revert to ordinary food, simultaneously increasing the quantity given. From about a week after whelping until the puppies are weaned the dam will be fed lavishly with plenty of flesh (raw meat, stewed beef, ox-cheek, offal, sheep's head, paunch, fish, etc.), milk feeds of various kinds, eggs, broth, wholemeal food and vegetables. She also has calcium and cod liver oil, or similar additives.

If the litter is a large one I give three meat feeds and two milk meals during this period. If there are only a few puppies less food will be required, but this must be judged by the bitch's and the puppies' condition and her milk supply. Leave fresh water always available as nursing mothers require ample liquids.

Weaning the Litter
I like to start weaning puppies early to lessen the strain on the dam, and also to make this as gradual a process as possible. Scraped raw beef and enriched milk can be offered at the third week, and at four weeks puppies can be having two small feeds of each of these each day. Other items are then introduced gradually: cooked meat of various kinds, fish, and a variety of milk feeds, plus fine puppy meal or crumbled wholemeal bread. I also add cod-liver oil and calcium or their equivalents daily.

At five weeks mine have five meals a day, three of meat and two milk meals and I continue this until they are eight or ten weeks old. At five weeks I consider puppies to be fully weaned, but the dam is still allowed to visit them if she wishes to, but is never compelled to be with them. In fact from the time of the birth the dam is always free to get out of the box and away from the puppies if she wishes to do so.

Worming and Other Matters
Puppies should be wormed at least twice before sale, and

they should not go to their new homes younger than eight weeks old. They should always be accompanied by a diet chart and instructions as to correct care and routine should also be given to the new owner.

Some breeds seem especially subject to worms despite every possible precaution. With my breed I find it necessary to dose at about three weeks old and again ten days later, with perhaps a third worming at about eight weeks old. But other breeds appear to be less susceptible, and it may be possible to defer the first worming until five or six weeks old, followed by a second dose a week or so later. One point I have observed is that puppies from maiden or young bitches seem to be much more liable to heavy worm infestation, and that as the dams grow older their progeny do not seem to be affected to the same degree.

Indications of worm infestation in young puppies are coat standing on end, hard and distended stomach, un-healthy motions, passing jelly or mucus, and a lack of weight gain. These symptoms may develop at a very early age and it is then advisable to dose without delay. The modern preparations are safe and effective and no fasting is required, and I have found no risk or danger involved in the treatment. Worming does not give puppies permanent immunity but they should remain clear for some weeks, although it may be advisable to repeat the treatment when they are about four months old, and subsequently as and when it appears necessary.

A further point is to keep puppies' nails short and they should be clipped each week to prevent them scratching the dam or catching in the bedding.

If tails must be docked and dew-claws cut these should be done a few days after birth. It is not a difficult job, but it is advisable for the novice to obtain the help of an experi-enced person to undertake this task. Care should be taken that tails are docked to the correct length as this varies for different breeds.

Some Aspects Concerning Dogs
Only suitable males should be used for breeding, and in addition to the same general requirements of good health

and temperament which apply to bitches, the standards required regarding type and quality should, if possible, be even higher. Fewer males are required in a breeding programme, so the elimination process must be even more stringent. With working dogs the same rules of strict selection should also apply.

Those dogs which do not measure up to the desired standard should not be used at stud, and it is a mistaken conviction to assume that every dog should be mated. Apart from other considerations this would not be practical, for numbers would get completely out of control in the dog population, with a rapid increase in 'also-rans' and unwanted puppies.

If a dog is used regularly at stud he generally falls into a pattern of life and does not worry unless a bitch is ready for mating. But a dog which is used only once or twice during his life tends to become awakened but not satisfied, and may well be more frustrated than if not used at all.

Most males settle down after puberty and do not worry unduly, but some breeds or individuals tend to be more highly sexed than others, and if a dog becomes an embarrassment the question of castration should be considered. This course is not generally necessary but in extreme cases it may be the best solution. The worried owner of an over-sexed dog may feel that if only he were mated it would calm him, but it will not generally solve any problems and as already suggested the condition will probably be aggravated.

So my advice is that you should accept that your dog will fall into one of three categories: firstly, top dogs to be used for breeding, secondly, other dogs which are kept for various purposes – as companions, as guards or for work. These dogs to remain entire, but not used at stud, and thirdly, dogs which are not suitable for breeding, but which are difficult and where castration may be advisable.

Care of the Stud Dog

A dog used regularly at stud must be kept in good condition, fit, hard and active. He should not be over-weight, but must be generously fed with a good proportion of protein in his

diet. The frequency with which a dog may be used will vary according to a number of factors. Perhaps as a rough guide, the smaller and medium breeds might average two matings a week during the dog's prime when between two and six years old, and this should not tax him unduly. With younger dogs, under two years old, perhaps once a week would be wiser, and the same would apply to those over six years of age. But such suggestions are subject to variation and must be elastic. I have known of dogs used much more frequently without apparent ill effects. With the bigger breeds it would not generally be advisable to use them as frequently as the smaller ones, but the question does not generally arise since they are not usually bred on a large scale in any case.

External considerations of management, handling, condition and the individual dog's potency, etc., must all play their part. If a dog is well cared for and is healthy and virile he may retain his fertility until he is in his 'teens; but this is unusual and not many dogs are still useful at stud after nine or ten years of age.

If a dog mates quickly and easily he can be used much more frequently than another, which requires several attemps to achieve a mating. The latter can lose more energy over one unsuccessful effort than the former would do in mating two or three bitches.

If a dog mates without trouble he will not be exhausted and will be as fit as before; after a little rest he will be ready to enjoy his food and be back to normal. If well managed a dog can be in regular use at stud and still keep in top condition for the show ring.

But conversely, the dog which steams about for prolonged periods, trying ineffectively until he is exhausted, panting and wild-eyed, and with his heart racing, will be far more spent. He is frustrated and upset and probably will not eat or rest, and these sessions if embarked on frequently will soon take their toll of a dog's condition.

The Mating
It is best to start a dog at stud when young as this is more likely to ensure an easy mating, and this could be at about

ten months to a year old for a small dog and perhaps eighteen months or so for a large one.

It is preferable to commence a maiden dog with a steady and experienced brood bitch, as a nervy or snappy one can upset a youngster. A small, empty, enclosed area is usually best for the mating, where the dogs are not distracted, and where there are no obstructions to impede matters or to make the dogs inaccessible if help is necessary.

Usually two people should be present, one to concentrate on the dog and the other on the bitch. But sometimes with big powerful dogs or those which are obstreperous, extra help may be required to steady the animals.

The bitch should be on the lead so she is under control, but she should be allowed free play to encourage the dog, and meanwhile the dog should be allowed to make advances and to gain confidence. The bitch must be the focal point and the handlers should remain background figures. Encouragement and praise may be offered, but these should be given quietly so as not to divert the dog's main interest from the bitch.

On no account should the dog be scolded or curbed, and no anger or irritation should ever be apparent during a mating or potential mating. If the bitch is aggressive she must be controlled, but this must be done by calming and soothing her, and by firm handling, or if necessary by muzzling her, and on no account by roughness or violent actions.

It is most important that matings are carried out in a tranquil atmosphere so a dog retains his confidence. If he is subjected to harshness or to inconsistent treatment, or is frightened or upset in any way, he may become an un-reliable stud dog, easily discouraged, and reluctant to co-operate with his handler.

It is my considered opinion that many potentially valuable stud dogs are lost to their breeds, or have restricted opportunities because of mishandling, so it is very important to approach the situation sympathetically.

Sometimes a bitch may suffer from a stricture which makes the mating difficult, or even impossible, so if the dog appears to be striking correctly but does not achieve a 'tie', the bitch should be examined to test if the passage is clear. The small finger, first sterilised and then covered with a little petroleum jelly as a lubricant, should be gently inserted into the passage.

If the way is clear the finger will slip in easily, but if an obstruction is felt it will be necessary to stretch this, or break it down, to enable the dog to penetrate. This can generally be done by easing the finger in with a screwing action, gently pressing and twisting and working it to and fro. The stricture may consist of a strip of skin across the passage which will require stretching or breaking down, or it may be a thickened band ringing the passage which will need enlarging to allow a way through. If this treatment is carried out slowly and carefully it does not upset the bitch, but on no account must it be done roughly.

When the bitch shows signs of being prepared to accept the dog, by turning her tail, and if the dog tries to mount her, the handlers should be ready to assist if required. The one assigned to the bitch should steady her and should be prepared to hold her firmly with both hands should she jerk as the dog is mating her. Meanwhile, the other handler should be watching the dog, ready if necessary to give him some support if he shows signs of slipping away from the bitch before he has effected the mating. Once he is mated he should be kept on the bitch's back for a minute or two before being allowed to turn, as if not fully 'locked' he may come away if he turns too quickly.

With some of the smaller dogs it is customary not to turn them, but they are held on the bitch's back until the completion of the tie. With some of the larger ones it is usual to lower the dog beside the bitch as this seems more comfortable for many big dogs. But most make a complete turn and remain back to back during the mating, and this is the normal position. The length of the tie may vary from five or ten minutes to half an hour or more, but its duration has no relation to the results.

As they separate after mating I usually raise the bitch's hindquarters and gently tap the vulva which stimulates the contraction of the vaginal muscles. As the dogs part there is sometimes quite a back flow of fluid from the bitch, and I try and avert this as far as possible. Only a small amount of semen is required to fertilise the bitch but there is nothing to lose by taking what precautions one can!

If everything is normal with a satisfactory tie, one mating should be sufficient. But if there are any unsatisfactory aspects, such as the bitch coming into colour again, causing doubts as to the correct timing, if the tie was not a good one, or if perhaps she has a history as an unreliable breeder, then it may be wise to have a second mating.

If a bitch is difficult to get into whelp it is worth trying several spaced matings at three or four day intervals. Try the first one as early as possible, perhaps at seven or eight days; a second one at the normal time of perhaps eleven or twelve days, and another as late as possible, perhaps at fifteen or sixteen days. I have known bitches which do not follow the regular pattern, and which may require mating very early or very late to ensure conception, and this condition may be difficult to recognise and is only dis-covered and corrected by trial and error. But if a bitch is difficult to get into whelp it is worth trying varying the timing to endeavour to catch her at her most fertile period.

Sometimes there is a difference in height between the animals and it may be necessary to adjust this with a low platform. Usually it is the dog who requires raising, and a board (if necessary on blocks) may be used, preferably covered with a sack or a piece of carpet to give purchase.

Some breeders prefer to mate the smaller dogs on a bench or table and the dog soon becomes accustomed to this. Personally I prefer to mate them on the floor as I find it a natural sequence from the preliminary flirting, but this is an optional decision.

The bitch should be brought to the stud dog when she is ready for mating, and every effort should then be made to effect this. This is particularly necessary if a dog is young and valuable and likely to be in much demand at stud, for it is important to ensure he does not waste his energy and that he is not disappointed, which may undermine his confidence and determination. If a dog is brought in and out to a bitch which may or may not be ready, and if he is tried repeatedly and unsuccessfully, these abortive attempts

can be most damaging to his future career at stud. Whereas
if he is only introduced to bitches ready for mating and is
given correct assistance, culminating in a successful outcome, he is likely to be fully co-operative and ready to
tackle even the most difficult bitch, and he should become
virtually one hundred per cent reliable.

It is most important that the bitch is never allowed to
bite the dog, and this is even more vital with a youngster.
If a dog is roughly treated by a bitch in his early days, this
may affect him to the extent that he refuses to go near any
other bitch which even growls, so the handler of the bitch
must keep her under control and be sure that this does not
happen.

If a young dog mounts the bitch incorrectly he must not
be checked or restrained in any way but the bitch should
be manoeuvred around towards him, and he should still be
praised and encouraged. To check him would not imply
'Don't do it at that end – do it at this end' – it would
simply mean 'Don't do that'.

I once had the greatest difficulty in handling a young dog
whose owner had been 'training' him by giving him a slap
every time he tried to mount the bitch at the wrong angle,
at the same time scolding him and telling him what a silly
dog he was, and that was not the right way to do it.
Eventually I had to send her right away, out of his sight
and sound as he was thoroughly bewildered by her apparently wanting him to mate the bitch and then giving him a
smack when he tried to do so.

Sometimes a dog is shy and very reluctant to try to
mate a bitch if people are near, but he does eventually
succeed when running with her and while both are free. In
this event it is wise to go quietly towards them once they
are mated and to hold the dog gently, stroking and praising
him quietly, and making relaxed contact, so he becomes
accustomed to human proximity in these circumstances,
and he may thus be willing to accept help on a subsequent
occasion if the necessity arises.

Dogs running together may mate naturally sometimes,
but sooner or later there will be problems and it may not
be possible for the dog to effect the mating without some

assistance. Either there may be a big difference in size between the animals which will require adjustment, or the bitch may jerk away at the crucial moment and require steadying. So unless the dog will accept human help, there will come a time when he may fail, so it is important for the breeder to accustom him to being handled.

After the mating the bitch should be shut away quietly for a rest before she is exercised or travels, and I try to avoid her passing water too soon. The dog too, should be put in his bed to relax and unwind for a period, and he should not be returned among other dogs for some time until he has completely settled down, when he can resume his normal life. If he is returned too quickly among other males this may create tension and such mishandling may well precipitate friction.

Final Hints on Management

I have kept stud dogs for many years, and I do not consider that they should be treated any differently from other dogs in their ordinary life, and my experience is that if they are treated normally they will respond normally.

But there are certain aspects which require careful management, and it is important not to inflame possible latent jealousy by allowing situations involving tension to occur.

Well before a bitch reaches the height of her season she must be removed and kept completely away from all stud dogs. If several dogs are running together and are able to see, or sniff, a bitch in season this will understandably cause friction, and possibly aggression and trouble.

I always run my dogs together, and have had as many as six or seven or more mature males mixing freely with each other and an equal number of bitches, all happy and friendly together, and I think when this can be managed dogs are much more contented and well adjusted.

It is sometimes considered that a stud dog must not mix with bitches or he will not mate them, but this has not been my experience, and I have had many very successful stud dogs who have lived as family pack dogs.

But although stud dogs may run together under supervision and in open areas, they should never be confined in small enclosures without somebody in attendance.

Young males of the same age which grow up together may not agree well when mature, as neither may be willing to accept the dominance of the other. But I have found if I grow on one new youngster at a time there is not this problem, as he automatically falls into his position as the junior member of the pack, and is thus integrated into the group. The next new addition to follow on falls into line under him and so on.

But I must add that I would never introduce a new adult male into an established pack and I doubt if this would be acceptable among many stud dogs. Some would mix readily on neutral ground, but they would not willingly accept a strange dog into their home surroundings.

BETTY PENN-BULL

I cannot think of anyone in the world of dogs more capable of writing on the subject of breeding stock than Miss Betty Penn-Bull. Since she can remember Betty has always been immensely interested in dogs. Her literary background enables her to pass on her knowledge in an extremely readable way. Miss Penn-Bull's over-riding desire as a child was to own a dog, but she was never allowed one. Her ambition as a youngster was to make a career with dogs but this too received no support from her family and without any backing she proudly secured her first job aged seventeen. Betty was not able to count on any paid training. It included helping in the house to compensate for lack of experience. After eight kennel jobs gaining experience and having managed to save £35 to start her own kennels, she was fortunate in finding a stable for the equivalent of 25p per week. Single-handed and making every penny count, with trimming, puppy sales, breeding and the use of stud dogs, Miss Penn-Bull built up a strain of Kennelgarth Scottish Terriers who are second to none in the breed here in Britain and anywhere in the world where pedigree dogs are known. Miss Penn-Bull has, since these early days, never been away from dogs and dog shows. She has owned seventeen British champions and bred nine. Betty's home-bred Scottish Terrier Champion Kennelgarth Viking is the greatest top sire ever known, creating a record by siring twenty-three British champions.

J.C.

10 Common Illnesses, Recognition and Treatment BY MICHAEL STOCKMAN

It is not intended that this chapter should do anything other than describe what a healthy dog should look like and what steps should be taken if any definite change in that state of health should appear. It must be stressed that your veterinary surgeon is there to be consulted on any occasion where the trouble is outside the scope of your own capabilities and delay in obtaining professional advice may result in a worsening of symptoms and a more serious illness arising.

Before one can decide whether or not a dog is ill, it is first necessary to know the classic signs of health. In brief terms these are as follows:

a Bright, clear eyes.
b A healthy shining coat.
c A readiness for exercise.
d A good appetite.
e The passage of normal quantities of urine and droppings of normal consistency and colour.

Against this may be listed the signs of abnormality:

a Dullness of either eyes or coat.
b Lethargy.
c Lack of appetite.
d Excessive thirst.
e Excessive scratching.
f Vomiting, diarrhoea and excessive urination.

It is obviously impossible in a single chapter to deal with any but a few of the main problems associated with disease and this I intend to do in alphabetical series.

Accidents
These are usually associated with a painful collision with a car or vehicle, but may be the result of being kicked by a horse. Another accident is the scalded or burnt dog. All these should be examined by your veterinary surgeon as soon as possible and if it is necessary to move a heavy dog it is often possible to carry him on a large blanket. This will not only make the problem of weight much easier to cope with but will also keep the injured animal warm and

help to guard against shock. While on the subject of accidents, it is well to mention that the dog in pain may well react to human attempts to assist by biting. That the helping hand may be the one that normally feeds him is no guarantee of immunity, so approach the injured dog with care. If possible apply a stout leather collar and hold on to it while moving or examining the patient.

Allergies

Many proteins can give rise to allergic reactions which manifest themselves in general by swellings appearing in the skin especially round the face. These symptoms are often referred to under the name of 'nettle-rash' and in most cases disappear as quickly as they arise, usually without treatment. Occasionally it is necessary to give an injection of an anti-histamine drug to counteract the histamine which has caused the allergy.

The cause may be something the dog has eaten, a sting from a bee or wasp or even a vaccine injection. Whatever the reason it is possible that more serious symptoms may arise as a result of the allergic reaction taking place in the lining of the stomach or intestine giving rise to vomiting, diarrhoea or dysentery with passage of blood with loose faeces. Reactions may also take place in the respiratory system producing signs of asthma-type breathing. Both these latter conditions are extremely serious and need very urgent attention from the veterinary surgeon. It cannot be too often stressed that when some urgent condition is apparent it is normally much better to put the patient in the car and drive straight to the nearest surgery rather than waiting for a veterinary surgeon to be contacted on the phone and directed to you. With the advent of multi-man practices running modern hospitals, all the necessary equipment is there to deal with an acute emergency.

Anal Glands

These are two secretory sacs lying just below and to either side of the anal opening. They produce a vile-smelling protective secretion which in the wild dog presumably acted as a lubricant to the hard excreta formed by a dog which ate the skin and bones of its prey as well as the softer flesh. With softer present-day intake our dogs tend to pass a softer motion and as a result the glands' function is partially lost. This causes the sacs to fill up and stretch the overlying tissue, causing the dog discomfort and making him attempt to get relief by rubbing his bottom on the ground or chewing at his hind-quarters with resultant patches of wet eczema on the skin of the area. The cure in simple cases is by digital compression of the glands and most veterinary surgeons if asked will demonstrate the technique. If the later stages of eczema or abscessing have been reached the appropriate professional advice will have to be sought.

Bladder
The urinary bladder, as its name implies, stores the urine. Problems in this organ can be those of inflammation or cystitis with or without bacterial infection, stone-formation within the urine leading to either irritation or blockage of the outlet or urethra, or both conditions together. Correction of all these conditions is essentially the task of the professional man and, especially in the case of a blockage leading to retention, is urgent in the extreme, requiring a greater or lesser degree of surgical intervention. Cystitis itself may need treatment with bladder antiseptics and antibiotics, as well as adjustment of the diet in order to lessen the chances of recurrences. Urine samples are usually needed to assist in making a positive diagnosis and can easily be obtained from dog and bitch alike if the collection is left to the time at which the animal is most ready to relieve itself. Care should be taken that such samples are collected in dishes and bottles free from all contaminants such as sugar. The actual technique of collection is simplified if an old frying pan is used. In the case of the bitch, give her time to get started before sliding the pan into place, or she may well stop.

Ears
The treatment of inflamed ears is without doubt one of the least understood of all first-aid attention required by dogs.

It would, as a generalisation, be better if owners were to leave sore ears severely alone rather than attempt to put matters right themselves. The only action that I would suggest for 'home-doctoring' is the use of a little warm olive-oil poured into the canal of the ear in order to assist the dog's attempts to remove wax and other matter which tends to accumulate as the body's response to inflammation. Any attempt at mechanical cleaning, however gently performed, is almost certain to lead to painful and worsening damage to the highly sensitive lining of the external auditory canal. This in turn makes the dog scratch and rub the ear all the more and transforms the mild case into the chronic. There are so many causes of otitis that a proper examination and diagnosis must be made before effective treatment can be instituted.

Eclampsia
This condition occurs in the nursing bitch as a result of lowering of the calcium levels in the bloodstream. The usual time of appearance is about two to three weeks after whelping when the bitch is producing the greatest quantity of milk, but cases are seen from the last week of pregnancy onwards. The symptoms are characteristic, and include rapid breathing, muscular tremors, progressing to inco-ordination and collapse. Total loss of consciousness may be rapidly followed in untreated cases by death, and help should be gained with the utmost urgency.

Ecto-parasites
This category includes the four main outside invaders which attack the dog's skin, namely, fleas, lice, mites and ticks. All four are unnecessary and every effort should be made to remove not only the parasites on the body itself but also those which have temporarily detached themselves and are in bedding, kennel-walls and the like. The dog-flea can jump prodigious distances and is not fussy about the species to be used as a host; so it may well land on human skin as well as rabbits, hedgehogs and cats. There are numerous effective products on the market, but it is imperative that whatever is used should be employed exactly

according to the makers' instructions (which will usually
include warnings about keeping substances away from the
animal's eyes). Incidentally, unless the label mentions cats
specifically, it is better to assume that it is NOT safe as
cats are notoriously susceptible to parasiticides. Lice do
not move about with anything like the rapidity of the flea,
tending to crawl slowly if they move at all, but they are
equally capable of getting off the dog and hiding in cracks
and crevices. They are particularly fond of attaching in the
folds of skin at the rear edge of the ears and may well be
missed as a cause of the dog scratching at its ears. In the
cases of both fleas and lice as well as mites, the best method
of dealing with those which are off the dog's body in
kennels is to use a blow lamp on all surfaces before carrying out the usual cleaning with disinfectant agents.

Mites are the basic cause of manges. The common
sarcoptic mange (scabies) is capable of great resistance to
treatment even with the most modern of drugs. It most
frequently attacks the areas of skin with least hair on
them and these are obviously under the elbows and in the
groin. Spread is usually rapid to other parts of the body,
and also to human beings. Treatment under veterinary
supervision is essential. Demodectic mange is seen most
commonly in the short coated breeds and is associated with
congenital infection. The body seems to have some degree
of natural resistance to the mite and symptoms in the form
of bald areas are first seen at times of stress such as teething in the puppy, heat-periods and whelping in the bitch;
in other words the moments when the resistance is at its
lowest ebb.

Mites are also found in dogs' ears, the otodectic mange
mites, and these are much more common as a source of ear
irritation than is generally realised. It is usual to find that
the origin of the infection is a cat living in the same household, so it is advisable to treat the family cat if your dog is
found to have otodects.

Ticks are normally found in dogs exercised in fields and
do not normally attach in large numbers. They may be
removed by bathing in appropriate insecticides, but should
not be removed by physically pulling them from the skin;

a drop of ether may be used to persuade the offender to let go, but as many ticks are found by the dog's eyes, this may not be possible.

Eyes
It is as well to deal with the subject of eyes under two quite separate headings. The first can be dealt with very briefly as it concerns the eye-balls themselves, in other words the actual organs of sight. If at any time it should be suspected that a dog's sight is in any way disturbed or impaired, the animal should be taken as soon as possible to a veterinary surgeon and in many cases to one who specialises in opthalmology. There is no place whatsoever for any attempt at home treatment except in the event of a hot or corrosive substance being poured accidentally onto the surface of the eye. In most cases it is best to wash the eye immediately with warm water rather than trying to make up a physiologically correct solution of saline. Having removed to the best of one's ability the damaging substance, the dog should then be rushed straight to the nearest veterinary surgeon.

The eyelids themselves which enclose the conjunctival sacs around the eyes may well be rubbed or scratched by the dog as a result of inflammation of the conjunctiva (conjunctivitis) and it is amazing how much damage a dog can inflict on itself in this way, and treatment should aim at preventing further injury until professional help can be obtained. Simple bland ointments or eye-washes, suitable for use in human eyes, will be perfectly satisfactory for this purpose, but it is essential that these should only be considered as first-aid methods and no substitute for proper advice and treatment. Eyes are much too easily ruined for life to take any risks by adopting a policy of wait and see.

Fits
Any form of fit is a serious matter to the owner and, although often very rapid in both onset and recovery, is none the less frightening to witness, especially when it is the first time a fit has been observed. While the attack is in progress, the animal is best placed in a confined space to

reduce the chance of self-damage. It is unlikely that a dog
undergoing a fit will bite deliberately, but care should be
taken in handling on those occasions where some restraint
is necessary to avoid damage to the patient and property.
Once the fit has ended, a rest in a darkened room is advisable, and meanwhile veterinary attention should be obtained.
Different causes of fits can often be distinguished by use of
the readings of an electro-encephalograph and such assistance in diagnosis will enable the veterinary surgeon to
recommend an appropriate line of treatment or management of the individual.

Haemorrhage
Any bleeding from a cut surface should be controlled as
soon as possible without waiting for professional help.
Wherever it is practicable a pressure pad should be applied
by means of cotton wool and bandages. If the first bandage
does not stop the bleeding put another one over the top
rather than remove the first. If the bleeding on limbs is
severe, a tourniquet may be applied above the wound by
means of a bandage put on tightly. This is merely a first-
aid technique and veterinary help should be obtained as
soon as possible. Tourniquets should not be left on more
than ten minutes without being slackened and reapplied
nearer the wound if necessary. Other bleeding points such
as those on the body should be treated by holding a pad of
cotton-wool firmly in contact with the wound for some
minutes. Do not keep removing the pad to see how things
are going as this may well dislodge the newly formed clots.
If a wound needs stitching it needs stitching as soon as
possible, so do not wait till tomorrow, get help now!

Heatstroke
Under conditions of extreme heat which are sometimes met
with in the backs of cars held up in traffic jams, a dog may
well suffer from heatstroke as evidenced by vomiting, rapid
breathing, weakness and collapse. The body temperature
will rise considerably and treatment must begin immediately. Removal to a cool place is obviously the first step
and this should be accompanied by the application of cold

water to the head and body either by pouring it over the dog or by immersing the animal in a bath. As soon as the animal shows signs of recovery he should be encouraged to drink and meantime should be dried.

Kidneys

The functions of the kidneys are bound up with the elimination of body waste from the blood-stream via the urine. The kidney is a highly complicated filter mechanism. Like all specialised tissues, kidney cells once damaged or destroyed do not repair to their full efficiency. Once their function is lost, they are replaced by fibrous tissue which can take no part in the technical task of the kidney. Many old dogs suffer from varying degrees of nephritis or inflammation of the kidney. While much of this nephritis is caused by a specific infection with Leptospira Canicola, a great deal of extra stress is put on the organs by over-feeding, especially with protein, throughout the dog's life. A great number of dogs in 'good homes' are fed with some degree of over generosity. Giving three pounds of raw meat to four-month-old Alsatian puppies does no good to anyone but the butcher, and puts a tremendous strain on those organs which have to digest and remove the excess protein, in particular the liver and kidneys. This process repeated over a lifetime will inevitably cause harm. As in the case of cystitis, a sample of urine will be required for aiding diagnosis and it may well be that the veterinary surgeon will wish to take a blood sample to estimate the degree of damage present. Advice on treatment will attempt to ensure that the dog's diet is so adjusted to put as little strain on the kidneys as possible and various prepared diets are available on the market to achieve this purpose.

Poisoning

No attempt will be made to discuss this subject in any breadth. Suffice to say that any substance which can possibly act as a poison to a dog should be kept out of his way. If this policy fails and any poisonous substances are eaten by a dog, an emetic should be administered as quickly as possible. Washing-soda or a solution of salt and

mustard in water will usually do the trick, but even if
vomiting is induced, a veterinary surgeon should be consulted as soon as possible for advice as to what further
treatment is needed, if possible taking the packet or its
name for his information. If the animal is already seriously
affected, it is essential that body warmth be maintained
while help is being sought, in order to counteract shock.
In this context, blankets and hot-water bottles are commonly used. While on the subject of poisons, it is as well
to point out that the commonly held opinion that Warfarin
rat poisons are harmless to dogs and cats is entirely wrong.

Skin Diseases
Apart from the ecto-parasitic types mentioned elsewhere,
there are numerous forms of skin troubles. These include
ringworm and bacterial types as well as a host of non-
specific conditions. These are the plague of the average
veterinary surgeon's existence, and their diagnosis requires
considerable expertise. Do not try home cures unless you
are certain that you know precisely what you are dealing
with.

Stomach and Intestines
The whole length of the alimentary canal from mouth to
anus can be involved in varying combinations of inflammatory disorders. The obvious symptoms are vomiting,
diarrhoea, dysentery and constipation. The dog, being a
carnivore and having in the wild a tendency to scavenge
from the carcasses of dead animals, is fortunate in being
provided by nature with great ease in vomiting. If this
were not so, the dog would have a poor chance of survival,
and in many cases a single spasm of vomiting is nothing
out of the ordinary, only a response to a bit of injudicious
feeding. In most cases vomiting dogs will tend to drink
water to excess and it is advisable to remove unlimited
supplies of water from their reach. If boiled water with
glucose added (one tablespoonful to a pint) is made available in small repeated quantities most dogs will retain it.
If after a short period the dog has stopped vomiting it is
then reasonable to offer farinaceous foods in the form of

ordinary semi-sweet human biscuits or sponge-cakes for a day or two. If, however, the vomiting continues when glucose water is tried veterinary attention should be sought.

Diarrhoea may occur as a symptom on its own or, as is often the case, as a sequel to vomiting. Again some basic irritation of the bowel is usually the cause and starvation along with the availability of small amounts of glucose-water will often be sufficient to allow the inflammatory condition to subside of its own accord. If it should continue for more than a day or if blood should appear in either vomit or excreta, veterinary advice is essential. Some forms of acute gastro-enteritis produce a great deal of blood from both ends of the alimentary canal and are occasionally rapidly fatal. Professional help is therefore needed at once, whatever the hour.

Constipation is not normally a problem in the dog which is intelligently fed and exercised. It is usually associated with the ingestion of bones whether deliberately provided or scavenged. It is surprising how often well-meaning neighbours will throw bones over the fence to a dog. The safest rule to follow when feeding bones to a dog is to give nothing other than raw, beef, leg-bones. Cooking removes the gelatine and renders the bones more brittle. These are the sort that splinter and provide ideal fragments to penetrate the bowel and cause fatal peritonitis. When constipation occurs, as evidenced by excessive unproductive straining and sometime vomiting, liquid paraffin is the drug of choice and should be given at the rate of an ounce to a 40 lb dog. If this does not produce a rapid answer, get proper help.

While on the subject of the stomach, mention must be made of that violent emergency, torsion of the stomach and Bloat. The affected dog will show symptoms of acute distress with attempts at vomiting with no result. This is because the twisting of the stomach shuts off the cardiac sphincter at the entrance of the stomach and makes it impossible for the stomach contents to leave the organ in a forward direction. The abdomen becomes rapidly and enormously distended and the dog will very soon collapse. This is possibly the most urgent emergency that can be seen in the dog other than the road accident case, and no time should be lost in getting the animal into the nearest surgery or hospital for immediate remedial steps, preferably getting someone else to telephone ahead and warn that the emergency is on its way.

Throats

The sore throat syndrome may be the result of pharyngitis or tonsillitis, or it may be the result of traumatic damage by sharp bones or needles. One useful way of telling the difference is that dogs with inflamed throats and tonsils will show difficulty swallowing and make gulping movements frequently, while the one with needle stuck in its tongue will in addition paw frantically at its mouth. Either way, get professional attention and never make any attempt to remove needles and the like yourself. You are far more likely to push them on down the throat. Choking may be caused by a dog swallowing a rubber ball which lodges behind the molar teeth and occludes the windpipe. An attempt must be made to remove the object with fingers and by cutting the ball with scissors to deflate it, but this is usually very near impossible. Another common cause is the stick that is thrown for a dog to retrieve. On occasion the stick will land in the ground rather than on it and the dog will run head-on into the other end. This will often result in a nasty wound at the back of the mouth. If this happens, never ignore the occurrence; have the dog examined professionally immediately as, apart from anything else, this accident causes considerable shock to the dog.

Uterus

The bitch's uterus is prone to trouble more frequently than that of other domestic animals. This is a result of the very delicate hormonal balance obtaining in the bitch which causes her to suffer false pregnancies almost as a normal state. Unfortunately the theories that breeding from a bitch will have any effect on her future chances of avoiding either the changes of false pregnancy or the various forms of inflammation of the uterus (metritis, pyometra), are not founded on fact. The suggestion that bitches which have never had a litter are more prone to pyometra than those that have is based purely on the fact that a greater percentage of bitches are in the former category. Owners contemplating mating their bitches should forget the idea that it is for the bitches' good and think first of whether there is a potential market for the possible puppies or not.

Vaccination
Your own veterinary surgeon will inform you of the course of injections which he or she considers most appropriate for your dog or dogs. The diseases which are normally considered are Distemper, Virus Hepatitis and the Leptospira infections. A course of two injections given at the correct ages will give the best possible chance of conferring immunity, and the best advice is that you should consult your veterinary surgeon not later than when the puppy is eight weeks old. You will also get advice as to the correct timing of booster injections and it is unwise to ignore them.

Worms
Until recent years, the worm problem was confined to those types known as round-worms and tape-worms. Now however, there is an increasing incidence of hook-worms and some evidence of whip-worm. It is obviously important to know for certain which particular type is infesting your dog. For this reason it is important to ask your veterinary surgeon to identify a specimen if you are in any doubt as to what it is. Each type of worm needs a different treatment régime and this will include not only dosing the dog with the appropriate remedy, but also dealing with the possibilities of re-infestation. In the case of puppies suffering from the ubiquitous roundworm it is advisable to dose the dam both before breeding from her and once she has weaned the litter.

Finale
If it appears that throughout these notes I have been

leading you and your dogs straight into the consulting-room of your veterinary surgeon, I make no apology. When you own a dog or dogs for the first time make it a policy to find a local veterinary surgeon and consult him or her. After the consultation, follow the advice given. If you do you will soon build up mutual confidence and you will receive credit for any knowledge and expertise you will obviously gain. Knowing when you need help, and knowing when you need it urgently are the two pieces of knowledge which will give you the best chance of keeping your dog healthy. If it is at all possible make a habit of taking your dog to the surgery. Many veterinary practices now run efficient appointment systems and in this way you can see the person of your choice and get the greatest benefit of the full equipment of the practice.

MICHAEL STOCKMAN

I invited Mr Stockman to write this chapter for many reasons, but mainly because I know that for many years he has been very interested, spent much time, and worked very hard to get breeders and members of the veterinary profession to work together in every possible way for the good of the dog. Mr Stockman qualified from the Royal Veterinary College in 1949, and spent four years in the Royal Army Veterinary Corps in Germany and Malaya training war dogs as guards, patrols, and trackers. The rest of his professional life has been spent in a mixed general practice. He is married to a veterinary surgeon who, in his own words, does all the intelligent work in the practice. He first showed dogs in 1942 by handling for a number of breeders and exhibitors of Golden Retrievers, Irish Setters, and Bulldogs. He bought his first Keeshond in 1946, but only started showing the breed with any purpose in about 1960. Now, however, when business permits, he can be seen at most leading shows around the Keeshond rings.

J.C.

ENGLISH COCKER SPANIEL

The general appearance of the Cocker Spaniel is that of a merry, sturdy sporting dog. A Cocker Spaniel should be well balanced and compact and should measure about the same from the withers to the ground as from the withers to the root of the tail.

Head and Skull
There should be a good square muzzle with a distinct stop which should be midway between the tip of the nose and the occiput. The skull should be well developed, cleanly chiselled, neither too fine nor too coarse. The cheekbones should not be prominent. The nose should be sufficiently wide to allow for the acute scenting power of this breed.

Eyes
The eyes should be full but not prominent, brown or dark brown in colours, but never light, with a general expression of intelligence and gentleness though decidedly wide awake, bright and merry. The rims should be tight.

Ears
Lobular, set on low, on a level with the eyes, with fine leathers which extend to but not beyond the tip of the nose; well clothed with long silky hair which should be straight.

Mouth
Jaws should be strong and teeth should have a scissor bite.

Neck
Neck should be moderate in length, clean in throat, muscular and neatly set into fine sloping shoulders.

Forequarters
The shoulders should be sloping and fine, the chest well developed and the brisket deep, neither too wide nor too narrow in front. The legs must be well boned, feathered and straight and should be sufficiently short for concentrated power but not too short to interfere with the tremendous exertions expected from this grand little sporting dog.

Body
Body should be immensely strong and compact for the size and weight of the dog. The ribs should be well sprung behind the shoulder blades, the loin short, wide and strong, with a firm topline gently sloping downwards to the tail.

Hindquarters
Hindquarters should be wide, well rounded and very muscular. The legs must be well boned, feathered to the hock, with a good bend of stifle and short below the hock allowing for plenty of drive.

Feet
Feet should be firm, thickly padded and cat-like.

Tail
Tail should be set on slightly lower than the line of the back, it must be merry, and never cocked up. The tail should not be docked too long or too short to interfere with its merry action.

Coat
Flat and silky in texture, never wiry or wavy, with sufficient feather; not too profuse and never curly.

Colour
Various. In self-colours no white is allowed except on the chest.

Gait
There should be true through action both fore and aft, with great drive covering the ground well.

Weight and Size
The weight should be about 28 lb to 32 lb. The height at the withers should be approximately 15 in. to $15\frac{1}{2}$ in. for bitches and approximately $15\frac{1}{2}$ in. to 16 in. for dogs.

Faults
Light bone; straight shoulder; flat ribs; unsound movement; weak hocks; weak pasterns; open or large feet; frown; small beady eyes; undershot or overshot mouth; uncertain or aggressive temperament.

AMERICAN COCKER SPANIEL

The general appearance is that of a serviceable-looking dog with a refinedly chiselled head; standing on straight legs and well up at the shoulders; of compact body and wide, muscular quarters. The American Cocker Spaniel's sturdy body, powerful quarters and strong, well-boned legs show him to be a dog capable of considerable speed combined with great endurance. Above all he must be free and merry, sound, well balanced throughout, and in action show a keen inclination to work, equable in temperament with no suggestion of timidity.

Head and Skull
Well, developed and rounded with no tendency towards flatness, or pronounced roundness, of the crown (dome). The forehead smooth, i.e. free from wrinkles, the eyebrows and stop clearly defined, the median line distinctly marked and gradually disappearing until lost rather more than halfway up to the crown. The bony structure surrounding the socket of the eye should be well chiselled; there should be no suggestion of fullness under the eyes nor prominence in the cheeks which, like the sides of the muzzle, should present a smooth, clean-cut appearance. To attain a well-proportioned head, which above all should be in balance with the rest of the dog, the distance from the tip of the nose to the stop at a line drawn across the top of the muzzle between the front corners of the eyes, should approximate one-half the distance from the stop at this point up over the crown to the base of the skull. The muzzle should be broad and deep, with square even jaws. The upper lip should be of sufficient depth to cover the lower jaw, presenting a square appearance. The nose of sufficient size to balance the muzzle and foreface, with well-developed nostrils and black in colour in the blacks and black-and-tans; in the reds, buffs, livers, and parti-colours and in the roans it may be black or brown, the darker colouring being preferable.

Mouth
The teeth should be sound and regular and set at right

angles to their respective jaws. The relation of the upper teeth to the lower should be that of scissors, with the inner surface of the upper in contact with the outer surface of the lower when the jaws are closed.

Eyes
The eyeballs should be round and full and set in the surrounding tissue to look directly forward and give the eye a slightly almond-shape appearance. The eye should be neither weak nor goggled. The expression should be intelligent, alert, soft and appealing. The colour of the iris should be dark brown to black in the blacks, black and tans, buffs and creams, and in the darker shades of the parti-colours and roans. In the reds, dark hazel; in the livers, parti-colours, and roans of the lighter shades, not lighter than hazel, the darker the better.

Ears
Lobular, set on a line no higher than the lower part of the eye, the leathers fine and extending to the nostrils; well clothed with long, silky, straight or wavy hair.

Neck
The neck sufficiently long to allow the nose to reach the ground easily, muscular and free from pendulous 'throatiness'. It should rise strongly from the shoulders and arch slightly as it tapers to join the head.

Forequarters
The shoulders deep, clean-cut and sloping without protrusion and so set that the upper points of the withers are at an angle which permits a wide spring of rib. Forelegs straight, strongly boned and muscular and set close to the body well under the scapulae. The elbows well let down and turning neither in nor out. The pasterns short and strong.

Body
Its height at the withers should approximate the length from the withers to the set-on of tail. The chest deep, its lowest point no higher than the elbows, its front sufficiently wide for adequate heart and lung space, yet not so wide as to interfere with straight forward movement of the

forelegs. Ribs deep and well-sprung throughout. Body short in the couplings and flank, with its depth at the flank somewhat less than at the last rib. Back strong and sloping evenly and slightly downward from the withers to the set-on of tail. Hips wide with quarters well-rounded and muscular. The body should appear short, compact and firmly knit together, giving the impression of strength.

Hindquarters
The hindlegs strongly-boned and muscled, with well-turned stifles and powerful, clearly defined thighs. The hocks strong, well let down and parallel when in motion and at rest.

Feet
Feet compact, not spreading, round and firm, with deep, strong, tough pads and hair between the toes; they should turn neither in nor out.

Tail
Set-on and carried on a line with the top-line of the back, and when the dog is at work, its action should be incessant.

Coat
On the head, short and fine. On the body, flat or slightly wavy (never curly), silky in texture, of medium length, with enough under-coating to give protection. The ears, chest, abdomen and posterior sides of the legs should be well feathered, but not so excessively as to hide the American Cocker Spaniel's true lines and movement or affect his appearance and function as a sporting dog. Excessive coat or feathering shall be penalised.

Colour
Blacks should be jet black with no tinge of brown or liver in sheen of coat. Black and tans (classified under solid colours) should have clearly defined tan markings, at specified locations, on a jet black body. The tan may be any shade of cream or red; some black hairs or pencilling permissible but brindling will be penalised. A mere semblance of tan in any one of these locations is

undesirable, while a total absence of tan in any one of these locations will be penalised.

The locations of tan are as follows:

1. A clear spot over each eye.
2. On sides of muzzle; tan should not extend over and join.
3. On sides of cheeks.
4. On undersides of ears.
5. On all feet and legs, extending upwards towards knees and hocks.
6. On underside of tail.

Solid colours, other than black or black and tan, should be of sound shade.

In all the above solid colours a small amount of white on chest and throat, while not desirable, is allowed but white in any other location shall be penalised.

Parti-colours should have one or more colours appearing in clearly defined markings on a white background. Roans may be any of the accepted roaning patterns of mottled appearance or alternating colours of hairs distributed throughout the coat.

Weight and Size
Ideal height at withers for an adult dog should be 15 inches and maximum height 15½ inches. Ideal height at withers for an adult bitch should be 14 inches and maximum height 14½ inches.

Note: Height is determined by a line perpendicular to ground from top of shoulder blades, dog standing naturally with its forelegs and lower hind legs parallel to line of measurement.

Index

Accidents, 116–117
Allergies, 117
American Cocker Spaniel, 46–59
Anal glands, 117–118

Bee stings, 117
Bladder, 118
Bleeding, 123
Bloat, 126–127
Breed standards, 130–135
Breeding, 94–115
Burns, 116

Choking, 127
Clippers, 38
Coat care, 30–45, 51–59
Collars, 79
Conjunctivitis, 122
Cystitis, 118

Dew claws, 105
Diarrhoea, 125–126
Diet, 15–16
    Bitches in whelp, 103–104
Dysentery, 125–127

Ears, 118–119
Eclampsia, 119
Ecto-parasites, 119–122
Eyes, 122

False pregnancies, 127–128
Field training, 84–86
Fits, 122–123
Fleas, 34, 119

Gastro-enteritis, 126
Grooming, 30–45

Heatstroke, 123–124
House training, 69–74

Illness, signs of, 116
Inoculations, 128

Kidneys, 124

Leads, 79
Leptospira Canicola, 124
Lice, 35, 119

Mange, 120
Mating, 109–114
Mites, 120

Nephritis, 124
Nettle-rash, 117

Parasites, 34–35, 119–122
Peritonitis, 126
Pharyngitis, 127
Poisoning, 124–125
Puppies, 15–19
    Bedding, 68–69
    Diet, 15
    (See also Training chapter.)
Pyometra, 128

Scissors, thinning, 39
Scratching, 35
Shampoo, 34
Show preparation, 38–45
Showing, 88–93
Skin diseases, 125
Spaying, 94
Stomach and intestines, 125–127
Stud dog management, 106–109

Tail, docking, 105
Throat, diseases, 127
Ticks, 35, 120–122
Tonsilitis, 127
Training, 60–82
    for the field, 84–87

Uterus, 127–128

Vaccination, 128
Vomiting, 125–127

Wasp stings, 117
Weaning, 104
Whelping, 99–102
Worming puppies, 104
Worms, 128